COMING
OF
AGE

COMING
OF
AGE

Collected by
Candida Lund

THE THOMAS MORE PRESS
Chicago, Illinois

ISBN 0-88347-146-9

ACKNOWLEDGMENTS

Jacqueline Wolf, TAKE CARE OF JOSETTE
From TAKE CARE OF JOSETTE by Jacqueline Wolf.
Copyright © 1981 by Jacqueline Wolf. Used by permission of Franklin Watts, Inc.

Guy de Maupassant, "The Wedding Night"
From THE COLLECTED NOVELS AND STORIES OF
GUY DE MAUPASSANT, translated by Ernest Boyd.
Copyright 1922 and renewed 1950 by Alfred A. Knopf,
Inc. Reprinted by permission of the publisher.

Jane Alpert, GROWING UP UNDERGROUND
From pp. 49-50 "Swarthmore was...arrived in
paradise.", pp. 52-58 "It was my intention...why I
went." in GROWING UP UNDERGROUND by Jane
Alpert. Copyright © 1981 by Jane Alpert. By permission of William Morrow & Company.

James Joyce, A PORTRAIT OF THE ARTIST AS A
YOUNG MAN
From A PORTRAIT OF THE ARTIST AS A YOUNG
MAN by James Joyce. Copyright 1916 by B. W.
Huebsch, copyright renewed 1944 by Nora Joyce.
Definitive text Copyright © 1964 by the Estate of
James Joyce. Reprinted by permission of Viking
Penguin Inc.

Clare Jaynes, "The Coming of Age"
From O. HENRY MEMORIAL AWARD PRIZE
STORIES OF 1942, Selected and Edited by Herschel
Brickell, Assisted by Muriel Fuller, published by
Doubleday, Doran and Company, Inc. First appeared
in STORY Magazine. Copyright 1941 by Story
Magazine.

Gertrude Berg, "Let God Worry A Little Bit"
Reprinted with permission from the January 1962

Contents

*Indicates an excerpt from the book

To the Memory of
ANN CLARK

PREFACE

"When I was a child, I spake as a child, I understood as a child, I thought as a child: but when I became a man, I put away childish things." Ringing words of St. Paul, but he does not indicate when is "when."

Barring legal definition (certainly not carved in stone) at what point are we able to say that we have come of age? There is an elusiveness to the moment, possibly because ordinarily there is no single moment. What usually brings that turn in our lives is an aggregate of experiences.

In *Come of Age* by Clemence Dane, the protagonist, actually the poet, Thomas Chatterton, but known in the play as The Boy, cries out, "Let me come of age in pleasure and pain!" To come of age not knowing pleasure and pain is virtually impossible.

Some psychologists claim that today's children too soon reach maturity. Other experts assert that we prolong adolescence. Certainly we are witnessing an escalating teen-age suicide rate—in rural areas as well as urban and suburban, in affluent homes as well as ghettos, in religious homes as well as those without religion. Should such development lead us to believe that coming of age has become more difficult?

This anthology examines twenty-eight instances where the principals take steps, conscious or not, toward maturity. The selections cover different centuries, countries, races, sexes. There are, nevertheless, underlying characteristics repeated again and again. Playing an important part in attaining maturity are: decision-making, responsibility, achievement, pain, pleasure, questioning.

In these selections decision-making may be the most frequently reflected characteristic. I am reminded of the young social worker described by Bruno Bettelheim in *The Children of the Dream*, a study of children of the kibbutzim in Israel. She said to him: "Whenever I'm in the city, I feel grown up, but as soon as I return to the kibbutz, I feel again as if I were a child. So much is decided for me, so few decisions do I have to make on my own...."

Whether, in these pages it is Jade Snow Wong, the Fifth Chinese Daughter, deciding that she will go to college or Ben Hecht deciding that he won't, Shirley MacLaine deciding that she will dance, or Ingrid Bergman that she must act—the decisions are all steps leading to maturity.

Yet the other factors, too, appear again and again. The impact of responsibility shows in Gertrude Berg's helping save the family's summer hotel, in Jacqueline Wolf's acquiescence to her Gestapo-arrested mother's final directive "Take Care of Josette." Ingrid Bergman, Lilli Palmer and John McKee illustrate the impetus that achievement gives to maturing. Deep pain is a part of the growing up process for Richard Wright. The rewarding pleasure of friendship helps foster the maturing of Fred Uhlman's teen-age boys. Questioning the social order launches Jane Alpert on growing up underground, and the young Maria moves closer to maturity as she asks, "What does it mean to be a Pueblo woman?"

Why this anthology? I was encouraged by the reception readers gave to a previous anthology of mine, *Moments to Remember*. In that book I chose from the lives of more than fifty women incidents which I thought would give joy, or courage, or hope, or comfort, or laughter. In this book my focus is more restricted but as in the earlier work I have mixed some fiction with the factual. I do this because fiction is often autobiographical and because some "facts" only get written as fiction.

Coming of age is an evolutionary process. What is believed at eighteen may not be accepted at twenty-eight, but one would hope that at twenty-eight (and plus) there is sympathy still for the teen-ager. Although certainly flip and a generalization, there used to be current on university campuses the saw: "If you're not a socialist at eighteen, you have no heart; if you're still a socialist at thirty you have no head."

This collection is designed to be read by those who are coming of age and by those for whom it has already happened. It is about the human experience and the lessons that can be learned from it. If it can be said to have a single aim it is to increase sympathetic understanding.

Candida Lund
Rosary College
River Forest, Illinois

Spring, 1982

TAKE CARE OF JOSETTE
by Jacqueline Wolf

For ten years Jacqueline Glicenstein was an only child, a condition that she strongly resented. She loved her home in Epinal, in eastern France, a short distance from Germany, but she wanted a baby in the house.

When Josette, her baby sister, was born on July 5, 1938, three months after Jacqueline's tenth birthday, she was taken to visit her mother. She found her in a hospital room furnished with French provincial antiques. The baby's basinette was pink as were her sheets, clothes, and cheeks. Her mother said to Jacqueline, "This is my present to you. You always wanted a sister; this way you will never be alone." The words were more prophetic than intended.

Josette was never far from her older sister. The baby's portable crib was wheeled next to Jacqueline's side while she did her homework, while she ate, while she read. She was with her more than anyone else, so that it was not surprising that the first word that Josette said was her sister's name.

Even before Josette was born the ominous shadow of Hitler fell indirectly across Epinal. German refugees came to Epinal to live as they did elsewhere in France. In the year that Josette was born Hitler's army attacked Czechoslovakia and then Danzig in Poland. The following year, 1939, France and Germany declared war. Paul Glicenstein was mobilized, and his family, like all other families, were issued gas masks.

None of this prepared them for what was to happen later. In the summer of 1942 the Gestapo arrested the parents of Jacqueline and Josette, the first Jews to be thus treated in Epinal.

I HAD not seen Papa for over two years. I was to return to school and stay until mid-July, which marked the beginning of the summer holidays. We would leave that same week to rejoin Papa in Orange; he was not allowed to return to the occupied zone.

During the Easter holiday I spent much of my time at Maman Marie's. I was happy to see Josette, who glowed with health and happiness; she was too young to be aware of the changes in Epinal.

Jews had a curfew in the early evening and were allowed to shop only during certain hours in the daytime. Shop owners were forbidden to wait on us at any other time, although many did. One day, Maman and I entered a store ten minutes late, and the owner, who had known us for a long time, refused to wait on us. At first Maman pleaded that she needed only one item. The shopkeeper was adamant, and she actually took us by our elbows and propelled us out of the store. I was humiliated enough by having to wear the star, but this was intolerable. Maman was more furious than embarrassed. As she walked out the door she said, "The war will not last forever, madame, and someday you will regret this action."

Another Nazi rule required Jews to step off the sidewalk into the gutter to allow German soldiers to pass. Maman, a proud woman, had never complied with such a ridiculous regulation and had never been reprimanded. Maman was a strikingly elegant lady; perhaps even German Jew-haters were impressed by her lofty demeanor. One day, however, she and I passed an S.S. soldier who ordered us in French to step down; Maman simply ignored him and walked on. Furious, he shoved her to the ground. Coolly, she got up, took my hand, and started to walk again. He pushed her again, a little harder this time, and shrieked at her in German, "You are a Jewish pig." By then, a crowd had

formed around us. Maman got up again with the help of a
French gentleman, stepped back on the sidewalk, took my
hand again, and told me to stop crying. I guess the crowd
intimidated the German, who walked away, trying to appear unruffled. Maman's coat was soiled, her stockings
were torn, and her knees were trickling blood. We walked
home, crying silently. I resented being Jewish more than
ever that day, but at the same time felt guilty about that
resentment.

On April 28, I celebrated my fourteenth birthday. I
thought, with hope, that the nightmare couldn't last much
longer. There was so much to look forward to: a safe life in
the United States, where Jews did not have to wear stars
and fear for their lives; seeing Tante Regine again. During
the remaining two and a half months of school the days
and the weeks dragged by, but Papa's letters of encouragement calmed my impatience.

Finally, the last day of school arrived, and I stopped in
Belfort as always. When I arrived at our friends' home, I
noticed strange papers, emblazoned with swastikas, pasted
all over the door. Although I spoke and understood German well, I couldn't read the printed German alphabet,
but I recognized the word *Jude*. No one answered when I
rang the bell, but eventually a neighbor came out and told
me matter-of-factly, "Oh, the Jews were all picked up by
the gestapo a few days ago." The Nazis had sealed our
friends' apartment, and the notice on the door warned that
anyone who broke the seals would be imprisoned. The
seals would remain on the door until the Nazis removed the
contents of our friends' home. My mind reeling, I walked
back to the train station, my stomach churning. I felt the
nausea that intense fear often produces. Would I find the
same seals on our front door? Had they taken Maman
away?

When I arrived in Epinal I was relieved to see Germaine, who rushed me home. The gestapo had not taken Maman away, she told me as we walked home, but Maman was in the hospital, where she was recuperating from an operation. Papa had been informed of Maman's illness and could no longer stay away. He was expected late that evening.

When he arrived, his appearance alarmed me. He was so thin; his hair was so white. I was almost surprised that he was able to hold me in his arms for so long and with all his old strength. I told him about our friends in Belfort, about my fear for our family. He told me not to worry because we would be leaving in the morning. We would pick up Josette and hide for a few days on a farm until Maman was ready to leave the hospital.

Papa and I spent much of the night packing. A friend of ours, Mr. Henriot, was to come at six o'clock in the morning to drive us to Maman Marie's.

In my parents' bedroom there was a traditional French armoire with a mirrored double door. In the frenzied activity of packing, Papa somehow broke the mirror. "Bad luck!" he cried. Papa was upset and knew, perhaps, that with or without the broken mirror, we were in for some bad luck.

Early in the morning, we went to bed. A short time later I was awakened by a loud knocking on the door. I jumped out of bed to open the door, thinking it was Mr. Henriot. To my horror, it was the gestapo: two German civilians, three armed soldiers, and a Frenchman from the Police Secrete who knew my father well. They pushed me aside and began to search the house. At that moment I knew that we were going to be arrested. I ran to Papa's room where he was dressing, his face drained of color and his hands trembling so that he couldn't button his shirt. He asked me to help, and I found myself able to do what he couldn't.

Meanwhile, the Nazis were ransacking our home, looking through all our things. Everything Papa had packed the previous night they scattered around the room. They asked Papa, "Where is your wife?" Papa just shook his head, as if he couldn't hear them, or couldn't understand. The French collaborator who accompanied the gestapo recalled that Papa always wore a watch with a gold chain on his vest. He kept saying, "Paul, where is your watch? Give it to me!" I remember Papa's incredulous and saddened look at this request. (After the war I pressed charges against this man, but dropped them when the Jews who remained in Epinal begged me to, since he was still in office and they were afraid of him.)

At one point, while the Germans were busy looking around, Papa whispered to me, "No matter how many times they ask you, don't tell them that Maman is in the hospital." Later, they hustled us out the door. Papa held back, but one of the men grabbed him and yelled, "Hurry! Get out, Jew!" Was this actually happening to us? It seemed as if an eternity had passed since Papa had come home for the first time in two and a half years, yet it was only seven hours before. When we reached the sidewalk it seemed that in spite of the early hour every neighbor had come out to say good-bye. Some women were crying, many shouted encouraging words to us, others cursed the Germans. There were two black gestapo cars waiting for us. The Germans attempted to separate me from Papa, but I held on tò him so tightly that they could not pull me away. Papa said, "Leave her alone; she is only a child." (I don't want to suggest that the Germans allowed me to go with Papa because they were moved by my tears. Never!

They were fanatically indoctrinated to hate Jews so much that a Jewish child was not a child but just another Jew who must be destroyed.) The reason I was able to stay with Papa was probably that the crowd was getting larger and louder, and the Germans were more interested in taking care of the business at hand than in coping with an angry mob.

Papa and I did not speak but just held on to each other until we reached the Commissariat de Police, Epinal's central police station. We entered the main room, which was filled with uniformed policemen and plainclothesmen, most of whom knew Papa. I sensed an attitude on the part of the French police, as if they felt guilty and embarrassed to be even indirectly involved in such a situation.

Papa and I were separated and taken to small offices. An officer questioned me about Maman's whereabouts, but I told them I did not know, that my parents had had a fight and that Maman had stormed out of the house. I told the same story again and again. The gestapo officer was getting angry at his French interpreter because the Frenchman was not insistent enough with me. All I cared about was to be reunited with Papa; I was afraid they would beat him. I was finally told I could join him in the main room. Incredible as it may seem, without consulting with each other, we had both told our interrogators the same story. Papa and I spoke for some time, but all I recall is that Papa thought we would not be released. He kept saying that if he had been able to get home sooner we would not be here. "What will happen to you, *ma cherié?*" Tears spilled down his face. Papa gave me a large sum of money and told me to hide it in my clothing and not to let anyone know I had it. He kept some in his own pocket so as not to raise suspicions in the event of a body search.

Only French policemen were in the room at the time, and they hardly spoke to us. I guess that they were helpless and stunned, and I think they respected our sorrow and understood our need for thóse few precious moments together. A car pulled up, and then we heard footsteps coming toward us. When I looked up I almost screamed, for it was Maman, flanked by two of the gestapo. This was the first time she had seen Papa in two and a half years, and she ran over to hold him close to her. The translator waved them on, into another office, and I was left by myself, hoping we would be released. I later found out that the gestapo had questioned all our neighbors and that someone had revealed Maman's whereabouts.

As soon as my parents came out of the other room, the Germans took them out of the police station but simply ignored me. I followed and ran along with my parents. They kissed me, and Papa told me to be good and never to forget them. As a German hustled them into a parked car, Maman pushed back the Nazi who was holding her arm as if to say, "You can do what you want with me, but I am going to kiss my child whether you like it or not." I saw reflected in her black eyes the fierce love she felt for her daughters, and then she kissed me. She kissed me with more tenderness than she had ever shown me before. As she entered the car, she turned and said, "Please take care of Josette, and don't forget your parents."

Why were they leaving? Why was I left behind? As the car drove away, I kept thinking, this is a nightmare; I *am* going to wake up. I shivered in the cold summer rain and watched the car make a right turn on to the bridge and disappear.

I knew then that the horror for me had begun. I had not

said a word as I stood there on the sidewalk. I felt a hand
touching me, so I looked up and met the sympathetic eyes
of a young man. Around him stood many of Epinal's
police officers, numb with shock. You see, my parents had
another distinction: they were the first two Jews in Epinal
to be arrested by the Germans. Many others would soon
meet the same fate.

The young man put his arm around me and led me back
into the building. It was July 13, 1942. I was too stunned to
be afraid. I felt more like a robot than a young girl whose
world had exploded. I sat where I was told to sit, and
above the murmur of soothing voices around me I kept
hearing Maman's voice: "Take care of Josette...take care
of Josette...take care of Josette."

THE WEDDING NIGHT
by Guy de Maupassant

Guy de Maupassant lived a short but creatively active life, dying in his early forties. He was an intimate of Zola, and was considered the most brilliant of his group. Though he wrote novels, he is best remembered for his short stories.

The French have never given themselves particularly to the short story as a literary form, but de Maupassant would have been considered a master in any competition. Indeed, many of his short stories—he wrote 300 of them—are considered unsurpassed. A sober and precise realist, "he portrays his characters as unhappy victims of their greed, desire, or vanity, but presents even the most sordid detail of their lives without sermonizing." Even with no intent to preach, his stories, "The Necklace" and "The Piece of String" have taught many a schoolchild lessons that have stayed with them throughout their lives. His characters often elicit a feeling of sympathy from his readers—possibly because one frequently finds something of one's self in the tales.

The bride in "The Wedding Night" is typical of her nineteenth century era—a child bride no matter her age.

MY dear Genevieve, you ask me to tell you about my wedding journey. How do you think I dare? Ah! Sly one, who had nothing to tell me, who even allowed me to guess at nothing—but there! Nothing from nothing!

Now you have been married eighteen months, yes, eighteen months, you, my best friend, who formerly said you could conceal nothing from me, and you had not the charity to warn me! If you had only given the hint! If you had only put me on my guard! If you had put one little simple suspicion in my soul, you might have hindered me from making the egregious blunder for which I still blush and which my husband will laugh at until his death. You alone are responsible for it! I have rendered myself frightfully ridiculous forever; I have committed one of those errors of which the memory is never effaced—and by your fault, wicked one! Oh! If I had known!

Wait! I take courage from writing and have decided to tell you all. But promise me not to laugh too much. And do not expect a comedy. It is a drama.

You recall my marriage. I was to start the same evening on my wedding journey. Certainly I did not at all resemble Paulette, whom Gyp tells us about in that droll account of her spiritual romance called *About Marriage*. And if my mother had said to me, as Mme. d'Hautretan did to her daughter: "Your husband will take you in his arms—and—" I should certainly not have responded as Paulette did, laughing: "Go no farther, Mamma, I know all that as well as you."

As for me, I knew nothing at all, and Mamma, my poor mamma, who is always frightened, dared not broach the delicate subject.

Well then, at five o'clock in the evening, after the collation, they told us that the carriage was waiting. The guests had gone; I was ready. I can still hear the noise of the trunks on the staircase and the blowing of Papa's nose, which seemed to indicate that he was weeping. In embracing me the poor man said: "Good courage! as if I were going to have a tooth pulled. As for Mamma, she was a fountain. My husband urged me to hasten these painful adieux, and I was myself all in tears, although very happy. That is not easy to explain but is entirely true. All at once I felt something pulling at my dress. It was Bijou, wholly forgotten since morning. The poor beast was saying adieu to me after his fashion. This gave my heart a little blow, and I felt a great desire to embrace my dog. I seized him (you remember he is as large as a fist) and began to devour him with kisses. I love to caress animals. It gives me a sweet pleasure, causing a kind of delicious shiver.

As for him, he was like a mad creature; he waved his paws, licked me and nibbled, as he does when he is perfectly content. Suddenly he took my nose in his teeth, and I felt that he had really bitten me. I uttered a little cry and put the dog down. He had bitten, although only in play. Everybody was disturbed. They brought water, vinegar and some pieces of linen. My husband himself attended to it. It was nothing, after all, but three little holes which his teeth had made. At the end of five minutes the blood was stopped and we went away.

It had been decided that we should go on a journey through Normandy for about six weeks.

That evening we arrived at Dieppe. When I say evening, I mean midnight.

You know how I love the sea. I declared to my husband that I could not retire until I had seen it. He appeared very contrary. I asked him, laughing, if he was sleepy.

He answered: "No my dear, but you must understand that I would like to be alone with you."

I was surprised. "Alone with me?" I replied. "But you have been alone with me all the way from Paris in the train."

He laughed. "Yes—but—in the train—that is not the same thing as being in our room."

I would not give up. "Oh well," I said, "we shall be alone on the beach, and that is all there is to it!"

Decidedly he was not pleased. He said: "Very well, as you wish."

The night was magnificent, one of those nights which brings grand, vague ideas to the soul—more sensations than thoughts, perhaps—that brings a desire to open the arms as if they were wings and embrace the heavens, but how can I express it? One always feels that these unknown things can be comprehended.

There was a dreaminess, a poesy in the air, a happiness of another kind than that of earth, a sort of infinite intoxication which comes from the stars, the moon, the silver, glistening water. These are the best moments of life. They are a glimpse of a different existence, an embellished, delicious existence; they are the revelation of what could be, of what will be, perhaps.

Nevertheless, my husband appeared impatient to return. I said to him: "Are you cold?"

"No."

"Then look at the little boat down there which seems asleep on the water. Could anything be better than this? I would willingly remain here until daybreak. Tell me, shall we wait and see aurora?"

He seemed to think that I was mocking him and very soon took me back to the hotel by force! If I had known! Oh, the poor creature!

When we were once alone I felt ashamed, constrained, without knowing why. I swear it. Finally I made him go into the bathroom while I got into bed.

Oh, my dear, how can I go further? Well, here it is! He took, without doubt, my extreme innocence for mischief, my extreme simplicity for profligacy, my confident, credulous abandon for some kind of tactics and paid no regard to the delicate management that is necessary in order to make a soul wholly unprepared comprehend and accept such mysteries.

All at once I believe he lost his head. Then fear seized me; I asked him if he wished to kill me. When terror invades, one does not reason or think further; one is mad. In one second I had imagined frightful things. I thought of various stories in the newspapers, of mysterious crimes, of all the whispered tales of young girls married to miserable men! I fought, repulsed him, was overcome with fright. I even pulled a wisp of hair from his mustache and, relieved by this effort, I arose, shouting: "Help! help!" I ran to the door, drew the bolts and hurried, nearly naked, downstairs.

Other doors opened. Men in night apparel appeared with lights in their hands. I fell into the arms of one of them, imploring his protection. He made an attack upon my husband.

I knew no more about it. They fought and they cried; then they laughed, but laughed in a way you could never imagine. The whole house laughed, from the cellar to the garret. I heard in the corridors and in the rooms about us explosions of gaiety. The kitchenmaids laughed under the roof, and the bellboy was in contortions on his bench in the vestibule.

Think of it! In a hotel!

Soon I found myself alone with my husband, who made me some summary explanations, as one explains a surgical operation before it is undertaken. He was not at all content. I wept until daylight, and we went away at the opening of the doors.

* * *

GROWING UP UNDERGROUND
by Jane Alpert

Because the means used by the young radicals of the Sixties and the Seventies were at times so horrendous, the "why" of their actions became obscured.

Jane Alpert, Class of '67 and honors graduate of Swarthmore, was attracted to radicalism in college, with its appeal intensifying after graduation. In late 1969, as protests against the Vietnam War escalated, she was arrested and charged with bombing a number of government and corporate buildings. She pleaded guilty to a charge of conspiracy. Six months later, however, she jumped bail and became a fugitive.

Then began years of life underground. She considered herself to be working toward a revolution that would end the war and bring about a society free of racism and economic inequality. Later she wrote, "I still needed a system of thought that was both revolutionary and comprehensive. I couldn't tolerate any form of ambivalence or the idea that there was no solution to the horrors I saw in the world. This need had led me into the radical left in 1969 and into radical feminism in 1972."

A certain disenchantment, however, took hold. She wanted to put behind her a life of aliases, furnished rooms and meeting her family and friends in motels.

Four-and-a-half years after the day that she had jumped bail, Jane Alpert, with her parents and attorney, appeared at the U. S. Attorney's office to give herself up. She served two years in jail, and was released in September, 1976. Since then she has lived in Greenwich Village, supporting herself by editing and writing. She has remained a feminist,

and sees feminism not as an ideology but as a way to work
for those social changes about which she cares most.
   Her autobiography bears this dedication:
      This book is for my parents,
      who never stopped helping.

SWARTHMORE was idyllically lovely. An uphill path, shaded with velvety pines, led from the train station to Parrish Hall, the Victorian manor that served as the administration building. Maple leaves were turning red and ocher. Men and women, absorbed in conversation, walked together on the graveled paths or sprawled on the grass, playing guitars or reading. A garden bloomed in back of Parrish Hall, filling offices and classrooms with the fragrance of roses. The Crum, a hundred acres of woods and meadow adjoining the campus, was alive with squirrels and sparrows and leafy spots for sunbathing or talk. For the first few weeks of September the weather was golden, and college seemed more like summer camp than work. I made friends easily, went to movies and recitals and poetry readings, and floated from impromptu folk singing to picnics to introductory lectures, convinced I had arrived in paradise.

* * *

It was my intention, when I came to Swarthmore, to join the Political Action Club (SPAC), an organization of campus New Left activists. Instead, I worked for the campus newspaper, the *Phoenix*, and the literary magazine, the *Roc*, and kept postponing my plans to attend a SPAC meeting. Editing, composing headlines, criticizing student poetry, and writing an occasional article on campus affairs came more easily to me than political discussions with the well-read social science majors who made up the membership of SPAC, whose arguments I had trouble following and whose arrogance intimidated me. Still, I admired the SPACers. Several of them had spent the summer working with SNCC in the integration movement in Cambridge, Maryland, where they had been tear-gassed by the National Guard and attacked by red-neck mobs. In October, when the administration invited a representative of the Union of South Africa, an advocate of apartheid, to speak on campus, SPAC members called for pickets around the lecture hall and organized a walkout in the middle of the speech. Nonradical students criticised the SPACers for their opposition to free speech, but I was proud to carry an "End Apartheid" placard in the demonstration.

Through the fall of 1963 SPAC members were devoting several days each week to work with a black mobilizing committee in Chester, a town three miles from Swarthmore. A community of about 60,000 on the Delaware River, Chester had been a major shipbuilding center during the war but had fallen on hard times in the fifties. Poverty and unemployment were especially severe in the black community. I saw the town several times on trips—not for political meetings but to eat cheese steak hoagies at Stacky's, an Italian-run sandwich shop in the black ghetto. The dilapidated houses and sleazy bars reminded me of the desolate inner city of Washington, D.C., where my grandmother and uncles operated their business, complaining constantly about the *shvartzehs*. When SPAC called for a demonstration to protest conditions at Franklin Elementary School, in the heart of the Chester ghetto, I was ready to go. It seemed an opportunity I'd been waiting for since I heard of the freedom riders.

Early Tuesday morning, November 12, nearly seventy-five students assembled next to Parrish Hall for the SPAC-chartered bus ride to Chester. Less than half were SPAC activists. The rest were freshmen like me who had not attended more than one SPAC meeting but had admired civil rights demonstrators for years and felt the time had come to take sides. Extra cars were pressed into service. A dozen students had to wait for the bus to return from Chester for a second trip. Lissa and I sat next to each other, too nervous to talk much, and looked out the window for our first glimpse of Franklin School.

Few of us realized that the militant tactics advocated by SPAC leaders differed from the civil disobedience methods employed in protests in the South. On the other hand, SPAC's publicity efforts had made the facts about Franklin School familiar to us. The school had been built in 1912 to accommodate five hundred students. It now held more than a thousand, all of them black. Classes were held in a former coalbin and in the boiler room of a housing project across the street. The school building had been declared a fire hazard by local building contractors. Children had been injured on broken stairs and worn-out playground equipment. The week before a group called the Chester Committee For Freedom Now (CFFN) had gone to court, seeking an injunction under state antisegregation statutes to close the school and transfer the students to safe (i.e., all-white) schools elsewhere in Chester. Our job was to make sure that the committee achieved its goal.

When we reached the school, two hundred Chester residents, overwhelmingly black, were guarding the entrances, arms linked as a symbol of unity. Others were milling around the yard. As children arrived, they were directed to the housing project across the street, where

SPAC chairman Carl Wittman and other Swarthmore students were conducting children's classes in black history. Preferring the potential drama of the picket line to baby-sitting, I squeezed myself into the front line around the school and watched as our ranks continued to swell.

At nine-thirty official word came from the school board: we had succeeded in closing the school for the day. Loud cheers, hugs, and handshakes. Then Stanley Branche, the black founder and chairman of CFFN, announced he was going to the school board to present the community's demands. Did we want to go with him? The crowd responded with buoyant approval. A few minutes later we were advancing on Chester's business district.

On that brisk fall morning under a strong sun, linked on the left to a middle-aged black man in work clothes, on the right to a young Franklin School student, I glimpsed the utopia preached by Martin Luther King: a culture in which all were equal, in which no one was made to feel inferior because of skin color or poverty or age or disability, in which a neighbor was someone whose arm you could hold. As we sang freedom songs, tears came to my eyes from the wind and the emotion I felt.

At the school board Branche disappeared for a long time. The crowd grew restless. Some talked of picketing Larkin School, one of the institutions to which CFFN wanted the Franklin School children transferred. The idea, springing from the moment's frustration rather than from planning, made me uneasy. I was relieved when Branche emerged from his meeting. The school board members had refused to negotiate. We were to go home for the day but return to Franklin School tomorrow. We would continue the picketing until they were ready to talk.

Back at the college that evening, the day's demonstrations were the only subject of conversation. No one had been arrested yet, but Wednesday, said the experienced SPACers, would be different. If the school board continued intransigent, we should be prepared to fight. I didn't know quite what fighting meant in this context; neither did most of the participating freshmen. But I trusted the SPAC leaders and Stanley Branche and wanted to be part of their victory over an unjust school board. If that meant a day or two in jail, it didn't seem a heavy price to pay. Believing that my decision was rational and right (although still feeling a bit nervous over the outcome), I called my parents, hoping for their support.

My mother uttered a few incoherent phrases, then handed the receiver to my father. In tones he might have used to a recalcitrant employee, he ordered me to stay on campus and leave demonstrating to the others. Neither was interested in hearing about the conditions at Franklin School or about how I felt on the picket line and the march through Chester. Hurt and angry at their refusal to listen, I could only conclude that we had different political goals. I hung up with no intention of obeying them.

Wednesday morning, arriving once again at Franklin School, we found the crowd in a grim mood. Vandals had smashed 150 windows in the school building during the night. Seven young black children had been taken into custody for the crime, but most of the crowd seemed to think that segregationists were responsible. Still, the vandalism had accomplished the immediate goal of the demonstration: Franklin School was closed until the windows could be repaired. This would take at least the rest of the week.

Once again Stanley Branche proposed that we march behind him, this time to the mayor's office. Why the mayor? Someone explained that as the hand-picked candidate of the Republican machine that controlled the town, the mayor was a symbol of the corruption and racism we were demonstrating against. We swept down the street, heading for the municipal building, a block or two from the end of yesterday's march.

What happened next had as much in common with the urban riots of the later part of the decade as with the pacifist resistance of the early civil rights movement. The crowd was angry and inclined toward anarchy and was led by a man who showed little disposition to moderate the tumult. We were nearly running through the streets of Chester, five hundred or more of us, singing "Turn Me 'Round" with such ferocity that reporters heard the words as "Burn It Down." At the doors of the municipal building the crowd hesitated only a few seconds before pushing through the double glass doors. The lobby resounded with our freedom songs. Branche was the last to enter. A husky ex-paratrooper who had once been a professional conga player, he timed his appearance perfectly, swaying his hips and shoulders in a sensuous two-step that mesmerized his audience. In a low, compelling voice, each syllable distinct, he led the chant. "Freedom! Now! Freedom! Now!" We picked it up in a frenzy.

I was prepared, or so I thought, for arrest, even for police brutality. But I was not prepared to find a wellspring of anger inside me, tapped by the chanting. As if hypnotized, I was frantically stamping my feet, cheering "Freedom! Now!" long after I was too hoarse to make a sound. I had stopped thinking about Franklin School, the citizens of Chester, the evils of racism and poverty. The utopian vision that had tugged at me yesterday was gone. In its place was something else, a fury that tore out of me with a life of its own, primitive as infancy. I was screaming against everyone and everything that had stood in my way—the boys who had rejected me, the man who had fired my father when I was nine, my absent father, my mother, my brother. I wasn't the only one in the crowd who temporarily lost control. When the police arrived, the entire mob sighed audibly, as at a long-awaited climax.

The men were taken to Broadmeadows State Prison. The rest of us, women and children, numbering about sixty altogether, were taken to a woman's detention facility in Chester. We were all jammed into two large bare rooms, one the dining hall and the other a recreation room for sentenced inmates—from whom we political defendants were kept carefully separate for the duration of our stay. The children under sixteen were released a few hours after we were booked. The adults (over eighteen) were told that bail would be set the next morning. Lissa and I, seventeen and sixteen respectively, were in a special category. We could be released only in the custody of responsible adults—and so we would stay in the jail until the college decided what to do about us.

I stayed up most of that first night, sitting at a long wooden table with a group of Chester women who played cards and talked. For me, these were the most illuminating hours in the Chester Jail. All the women around the table had been born and brought up in Chester. Most had children in the Chester school system. They lived near each other and were neighbors for years before CFFN was started. As I heard them talk about the problems of their neighborhood—not only the schools but their landlords and jobs and the illnesses of their children and parents—I began to realize that I knew pitifully little about their lives. For the first time I asked the questions I should have tried to answer before joining the demonstration in the morning. Was it good to have achieved the closing of Franklin School for an entire week, or would it only make the children suffer? Was Stanley Branche a selfless leader who had the community's interests at heart, or was he out for power for himself? Would the white college-student contingent in the jails ultimately help or hurt the civil rights with the voters of Chester? Was the school board really as intransigent and racist as Wittman and Branche wanted us to believe?

Thursday afternoon all the woman except Lissa and me were released. In the few hours we spent alone in the jail, we shared our anxiety over the classes and homework we were missing, the mid-term exams we would be unprepared for. Already far behind in three of my five courses, I was in worse difficulty than Lissa. Just as I was coming to regret my impulsive decision to join the demonstration on Wednesday, another two hundred demonstrators were ushered into the jail, singing as lustily as we had the day before. This group had not bothered to go to Franklin School, which was still closed because of the broken windows. Instead, they had created havoc in the municipal building until the police came. The point was to overload the courts and flood the jails until the government was forced to give in out of sheer exhaustion. Cathy Wilkerson, a Swarthmore junior and SPAC activist, boasted of how militant the demonstrators had been. One SPACer, Peter Grant, had leaped on top of the switchboard in the municipal building and pulled out the plugs with such undisguised glee that the switchboard operator took refuge under the board. Hoping to impress Cathy with my own fortitude, I mentioned that Lissa and I had been in jail more than twenty-four hours already—and added that I was thinking of avoiding future arrests until I reached the legal age of eighteeen. Cathy shot me a contemptuous look. Feeling reprimanded for having weakened so quickly, I kept my mouth shut around her afterward.

We stayed in jail until the following afternoon, at which point the school board, fearing yet a third day of miiitant demonstrations, yielded to virtually all of the community demands. It agreed to transfer 165 students from Franklin School to other schools in the district, to eliminate classes in the coal bin and in the housing project boiler room, to improve the toilet facilities, repair the concrete steps, and clean the playground. Finally the government had agreed, in exchange for a promise from Branche to end the demonstrations, to drop all charges against the demonstrators. The problem of how Lissa and I, as juveniles, would be released into adult custody was solved. We hugged each other, more in relief at getting out of jail than at the CFFN victory.

On the way to the courthouse we were singing again, but I choked on the words when I saw my parents standing outside the courthouse. After receiving the news from the Swarthmore deans, my father had taken a day off from work and my mother from teaching school to fetch me from jail. In spite of the doubts that had disturbed me in the women's jail, the sight of my parents made me ready to affirm everything I had done: the demonstrations, the arrest, and prison. I couldn't appreciate the fact that they had come out of concern for me. When I had needed them to listen, they had been short-tempered. Now I could take care of myself, and I hated them for trying to interfere.

My parents drove Lissa and me back to the campus. Lissa thanked them courteously, promised them she would call her own parents in New Orleans, and headed for the dorm. My father turned to me.

"I don't want to hear a speech from you," he said. "I told you what I expected and you didn't listen. I'm not going to warn you again. Wait until you're old enough to pay your own bills; then you can do whatever you damn please."

Cretins, I screamed silently at the departing Oldsmobile. At least you could have asked me why I went.

A PORTRAIT OF THE ARTIST AS A YOUNG MAN
by James Joyce

"Few writers have achieved acknowledgment as geniuses and yet aroused so much discontent and reproach as Joyce. To his Irish countrymen he is still obscene and very likely mad; they were the last of nations to lift the ban on Ulysses." *So wrote Richard Ellmann, Joyce's biographer, in 1959. Yet in 1962 a Joyce museum, containing pictures, papers, and first editions of his books, was dedicated in Dublin, and in 1982 the centenary of his birth was celebrated all over Ireland.*

Joyce, a master of language and radical literary techniques, has been acclaimed as the most significant writer of the twentieth century. A Portrait of the Artist as a Young Man *is highly autobiographical. It is the story of Stephan Dedalus (after St. Stephen, first martyr, and Daedalus, mythical figure who made wings for himself and his son). Dedalus realizes that before he can be a true artist he must free himself of what he looks upon as the shackles of religion and politics and the bigotry they engendered.*

With nimbleness Joyce cast off his own "shackles." He left Ireland for Paris (Shaw, Wilde and Yeats had gone to London; he would do something else). Two years later he returned to Ireland and on June 16, 1904—the day he was later to memorialize in Ulysses—*he fell deeply in love with Nora Barnacle. They returned to Paris and eventually married, living at various times in Paris, Trieste and Zurich.*

Nora, their two children and his writing were the passion of Joyce's life, a life often plagued by illness. When he was in his mid-thirties he contracted glaucoma, and for nearly

*a quarter of a century endured pain, near blindness and in-
numerable operations. Joyce was not an easy man with
whom to live. He once described himself as "a man of
small virtue, inclined to alcoholism." Ellmann speaks of
him as "the porcupine of authors," and tells of his "usual
impetuous quickness to discover enemies." For Nora his
greatness transcended his frailties. They gave happiness to
each other.*

*Joyce died in Switzerland. At his funeral a dramatic
touch of Ireland was provided by a green wreath with a
lyre, the country's emblem, woven in it.*

HE could wait no longer.

From the door of Byron's publichouse to the gate of
Clontarf Chapel, from the gate of Clontarf Chapel to the
door of Byron's publichouse, and then back again to the
chapel and then back again to the publichouse he had paced slowly at first, planting his steps scrupulously in the
spaces of the patchwork of the footpath, then timing their
fall to the fall of verses. A full hour had passed since his
father had gone in with Dan Crosby, the tutor, to find out
for him something about the university. For a full hour he
had paced up and down, waiting: but he could wait no
longer.

He set off abruptly for the Bull, walking rapidly lest his
father's shrill whistle might call him back; and in a few
moments he had rounded the curve at the police barrack
and was safe.

Yes, his mother was hostile to the idea, as he had read
from her listless silence. Yet her mistrust pricked him more
keenly than his father's pride and he thought coldly how he
had watched the faith which was fading down in his soul
aging and strengthening in her eyes. A dim antagonism

gathered force within him and darkened his mind as a cloud against her disloyalty: and when it passed, cloudlike, leaving his mind serene and dutiful towards her again, he was made aware dimly and without regret of a first noiseless sundering of their lives.

The university! So he had passed beyond the challenge of the sentries who had stood as guardians of his boyhood and had sought to keep him among them that he might be subject to them and serve their ends. Pride after satisfaction uplifted him like long slow waves. The end he had been born to serve yet did not see had led him to escape by an unseen path: and now it beckoned to him once more and a new adventure was about to be opened to him. It seemed to him that he heard notes of fitful music leaping upwards a tone and downwards a diminished fourth, upwards a tone and downwards a major third, like triple-branching flames leaping fitfully, flame after flame, out of a midnight wood. It was an elfin prelude, endless and formless; and, as it grew wilder and faster, the flames leaping out of time, he seemed to hear from under the boughs and grasses wild creatures racing, their feet pattering like rain upon the leaves. Their feet passed in pattering tumult over his mind, the feet of hares and rabbits, the feet of harts and hinds and antelopes, until he heard them no more and remembered only a proud cadence from Newman:

—Whose feet are as the feet of harts and underneath the everlasting arms.

The pride of that dim image brought back to his mind the dignity of the office he had refused. All through his boyhood he had mused upon that which he had so often thought to be his destiny and when the moment had come for him to obey the call he had turned aside, obeying a

wayward instinct. Now time lay between: the oils of or-
dination would never anoint his body. He had refused.
Why?

He turned seaward from the road at Dollymount and as
he passed on to the thin wooden bridge he felt the planks
shaking with the tramp of heavily shod feet. A squad of
Christian Brothers was on its way back from the Bull and
had begun to pass, two by two, across the bridge. Soon the
whole bridge was trembling and resounding. The uncouth
faces passed him two by two, stained yellow or red or livid
by the sea, and as he strove to look at them with ease and
indifference, a faint stain of personal shame and com-
miseration rose to his own face. Angry with himself he
tried to hide his face from their eyes by gazing down
sideways into the shallow swirling water under the bridge
but he still saw a reflection therein of their topheavy silk
hats, and humble tape-like collars and loosely hanging
clerical clothes.

—Brother Hickey.
Brother Quaid.
Brother MacArdle.
Brother Keogh.

Their piety would be like their names, like their faces,
like their clothes; and it was idle for him to tell himself that
their humble and contrite hearts, it might be, paid a far
richer tribute of devotion than his had ever been, a gift
tenfold more acceptable than his elaborate adoration. It
was idle for him to move himself to be generous towards
them, to tell himself that if he ever came to their gates,
stripped of his pride, beaten and in beggar's weeds, that
they would be generous towards him, loving him as
themselves. Idle and embittering, finally, to argue, against
his own dispassionate certitude, that the commandment of

love bade us not to love our neighbour as ourselves with the same amount and intensity of love but to love him as ourselves with the same kind of love.

He drew forth a phrase from his treasure and spoke it softly to himself:

—A day of dappled seaborne clouds.

The phrase and the day and the scene harmonised in a chord. Words. Was it their colours? He allowed them to glow and fade, hue after hue: sunrise gold, the russet and green of apple orchards, azure of waves, the greyfringed fleece of clouds. No, it was not their colours; it was the poise and balance of the period itself. Did he then love the rhythmic rise and fall of words better than their associations of legend and colour? Or was it that, being as weak of sight as he was shy of mind, he drew less pleasure from the reflection of the glowing sensible world through the prism of a language manycoloured and richly storied than from the contemplation of an inner world of individual emotions mirrored perfectly in a lucid supple periodic prose?

He passed from the trembling bridge on to firm land again. At that instant, as it seemed to him, the air was chilled; and looking askance towards the water he saw a flying squall darkening and crisping suddenly the tide. A faint click at his heart, a faint throb in his throat told him once more of how his flesh dreaded the cold infra-human odour of the sea: yet he did not strike across the downs on his left but held straight on along the spine of rocks that pointed against the river's mouth.

A veiled sunlight lit up faintly the grey sheet of water where the river was embayed. In the distance along the course of the slowflowing Liffey slender masts flecked the sky and, more distant still, the dim fabric of the city lay

prone in haze. Like a scene on some vague arras, old as
man's weariness, the image of the seventh city of Christen-
dom was visible to him across the timeless air, no older nor
more weary nor less patient of subjection than in the days
of the thingmote.

Disheartened, he raised his eyes towards the slowdrifting
clouds, dappled and seaborne. They were voyaging across
the deserts of the sky, a host of nomads on the march,
voyaging high over Ireland, westward bound. The Europe
they had come from lay out there beyond the Irish sea,
Europe of strange tongues and valleyed and woodbegirt
and citadelled and of entrenched and marshalled races. He
heard a confused music within him as of memories and
names which he was almost conscious of but could not
capture even for an instant; then the music seemed to
recede, to recede, to recede: and from each receding trail
of nebulous music there fell always one long-drawn calling
note, piercing like a star the dusk of silence. Again! Again!
Again! A voice from beyond the world was calling.

—Hello, Stephanos!

—Here comes The Dedalus!

Ao!...Eh, give it over, Dwyer, I'm telling you or I'll
give you a stuff in the kisser for yourself...Ao!

—Good man, Towser! Duck him!

—Come along, Dedalus! Bous Stephanoumenos! Bous
Stephaneforos!

—Duck him! Guzzle him now, Towser!

—Help! Help!....Ao!

He recognized their speech collectively before he
distinguished their faces, the mere sight of that medley of
wet nakedness chilled him to the bone. Their bodies,
corpsewhite or suffused with a pallid golden light or rawly
tanned by the suns, gleamed with the wet of the sea. Their

diving-stone, poised on its rude supports and rocking under their plunges, and the rough-hewn stones of the sloping breakwater over which they scrambled in their horseplay, gleamed with a cold wet lustre. The towels with which they smacked their bodies were heavy with cold sea water: and drenched with cold brine was their matted hair.

He stood still in deference to their calls and parried their banter with easy words. How characterless they looked: Shuley without his deep unbuttoned collar, Ennis without his scarlet belt with the snaky clasp, and Connolly without his Norfolk coat with the flapless sidepockets! It was a pain to see them and a sword-like pain to see the signs of adolescence that made repellent their pitiable nakedness. Perhaps they had taken refuge in number and noise from the secret dread in their souls. But he, apart from them in silence, remembered in what dread he stood of the mystery of his own body.

—Stephanos Dedalos! Bonus Stephanoumenos! Bous Stephaneforos!

Their banter was not new to him and now it flattered his mild proud sovereignty. Now, as never before, his strange name seemed to him a prophecy. So timeless seemed the grey warm air, so fluid and impersonal his own mood, that all ages were as one to him. A moment before the ghost of the ancient kingdom of the Danes had looked forth through the vesture of the hazewrapped city. Now, at the name of the fabulous artificer, he seemed to hear the noise of dim waves and to see a winged form flying above the waves and slowly climbing the air. What did it mean? Was it a quaint device opening a page of some medieval book of prophecies and symbols, a hawklike man flying sunward above the sea, a prophecy of the end he had been born to serve and had been following through the mists of childhood and boyhood, a symbol of the artist forging anew in his workshop out of the sluggish matter of the earth a new soaring impalpable imperishable being?

His heart trembled; his breath came faster and a wild spirit passed over his limbs as though he were soaring sunward. His heart trembled in an ecstasy of fear and his soul was in flight. His soul was soaring in an air beyond the world and the body he knew was purified in a breath and delivered of incertitude and made radiant and commingled with the element of the spirit. An ecstasy of flight made radiant his eyes and wild his breath and tremulous and wild and radiant his windswept limbs.

—One! Two!...Look out!

—O, Cripes, I'm drownded!

—One! Two! Three and away!

—The next! The next!

—One!...Uk!

—Stephaneforos!

His throat ached with a desire to cry aloud, the cry of a hawk or eagle on high, to cry piercingly of his deliverance to the winds. This was the call of life to his soul not the dull gross voice of the world of duties and despair, not the inhuman voice that had called him to the pale service of the altar. An instant of wild flight had delivered him and the cry of triumph which his lips withheld cleft his brain.

—Stephaneforos!

What were they now but the cerements shaken from the body of death—the fear he had walked in night and day, the incertitude that had ringed him round, the shame that had abased him within and without—cerements, the linens of the grave?

His soul had arisen from the grave of boyhood, spurning her grave-clothes. Yes! Yes! Yes! He would create proudly out of the freedom and power of his soul, as the great artificer whose name he bore, a living thing, new and soaring and beautiful, impalpable, imperishable.

He started up nervously from the stoneblock for he could no longer quench the flame in his blood. He felt his cheeks aflame and his throat throbbing with song. There was a lust of wandering in his feet that burned to set out for the ends of the earth. On! On! his heart seemed to cry. Evening would deepen above the sea, night fall upon the plains, dawn glimmer before the wanderer and show him strange fields and hills and faces. Where?

He looked northward towards Howth. The sea had fallen below the line of seawrack on the shallow side of the breakwater and already the tide was running out fast along the foreshore. Already one long oval bank of sand lay warm and dry amid the wavelets. Here and there warm isles of sand gleamed above the shallow tides and about the isles and around the long bank and amid the shallow currents of the beach were lightclad figures, wading and delving.

In a few moments he was barefoot, his stockings folded in his pockets, and his canvas shoes dangling by their knotted laces over his shoulders and, picking a pointed salteaten stick out of the jetsam among the rocks, he clambered down the slope of the breakwater.

There was a long rivulet in the strand and, as he waded slowly up its course, he wondered at the endless drift of seaweed. Emerald and black and russet and olive, it moved beneath the current, swaying and turning. The water of the rivulet was dark with endless drift and mirrored the highdrifting clouds. The clouds were drifting above him silently and silently the seatangle was drifting below him; and the grey warm air was still: and a new wild life was singing in his veins.

Where was his boyhood now? Where was the soul that had hung back from her destiny, to brood alone upon the shame of her wounds and in her house of squalor and subterfuge to queen it in faded cerements and in wreaths that withered at the touch? Or where was he?

He was alone. He was unheeded, happy, and near to the wild heart of life. He was alone and young and willful and wildhearted, alone amid a waste of wild air and brackish waters and the seaharvest of shells and tangle and veiled grey sunlight and gayclad lightclad figures of children and girls and voices childish and girlish in the air.

A girl stood before him in midstream, alone and still, gazing out to sea. She seemed like one whom magic had changed into the likeness of a strange and beautiful seabird. Her long slender bare legs were delicate as a crane's and pure save where an emerald trail of seaweed had fashioned itself as a sign upon the flesh. Her thighs, fuller and softhued as ivory, were bared almost to the hips where the white fringes of her drawers were like feathering of soft white down. Her slateblue skirts were kilted boldly about her waist and dovetailed behind her. Her bosom was as a bird's, soft and slight, slight and soft as the breast of some darkplumaged dove.

But her long fair hair was girlish: and girlish, and touched with the wonder of mortal beauty, her face.

She was alone and still, gazing out to sea; and when she felt his presence and the worship of his eyes her eyes turned to him in quiet sufferance of his gaze, without shame or wantonness. Long, long she suffered his gaze and then quietly withdrew her eyes from his and bent them towards the stream, gently stirring the water with her foot hither and thither. The first faint noise of gently moving water broke the silence low and faint and whispering, faint as the bells of sleep; hither and thither, hither and thither: and a faint flame trembled on her cheek.

—Heavenly God! cried Stephen's soul, in an outburst of profane joy.

He turned away from her suddenly and set off across the strand. His cheeks were aflame; his body was aglow; his limbs were trembling. On and on and on and on he strode, far out over the sands, singing wildly to the sea, crying to greet the advent of the life that had cried to him.

Her image had passed into his soul for ever and no word had broken the holy silence of his ecstasy. Her eyes had called him and his soul had leaped at the call. To live, to err, to fall, to triumph, to recreate life out of life! A wild angel had appeared to him, the angel of mortal youth and beauty, an envoy from the fair courts of life, to throw open before him in an instant of ecstasy the gates of all the ways of error and glory. On and on and on and on!

He halted suddenly and heard his heart in the silence. How far had he walked? What hour was it?

There was no human figure near him nor any sound borne to him over the air. But the tide was near the turn and already the day was on the wane. He turned landward and ran towards the shore and, running up the sloping beach, reckless of the sharp shingle, found a sandy nook amid a ring of tufted sand-knolls and lay down there that the peace and silence of the evening might still the riot of his blood.

He felt above him the vast indifferent dome and the calm processes of the heavenly bodies; and the earth beneath him, the earth that had borne him, had taken him to her breast.

He closed his eyes in the languor of sleep. His eyelids trembled as if they felt the vast cyclic movement of the earth and her watchers, trembled as if they felt the strange light of some new world. His soul was swooning into some new world, fantastic, dim, uncertain as under sea, traversed by cloudy shapes and beings. A world, a glimmer, or a flower? Glimmering and trembling, trembling and unfolding, a breaking light, an opening flower, it spread in endless succession to itself, breaking in full crimson and unfolding and fading to palest rose, leaf by leaf and wave of light by wave of light, flooding all the heavens with its soft flushes, every flush deeper than the other.

Evening had fallen when he woke and the sand and arid grasses of his bed glowed no longer. He rose slowly and, recalling the rapture of his sleep, sighed at its joy.

He climbed at the crest of the sandhill and gazed about him. Evening had fallen. A rim of the young moon cleft the pale waste of skyline, the rim of a silver hoop embedded in grey sand; and the tide was flowing in fast to the land with a low whisper of her waves, islanding a few last figures in distant pools.

THE COMING OF AGE
by Clare Jaynes

Conversational exchanges, excluding those within a family circle, between two touching generations are often perfunctory, sometimes painful. Likely, this is more disturbing to the not-yet-secure young, who expect more, than it is to their resigned elders. One needs only to recall the opening scene of The Graduate *by Charles Webb where Benjamin is driven from his own graduation party by the battery of meaningless remarks hurled at him by his parents' friends.*

Sometimes, even within a family, communications can be lacking. In his autobiography, A Better Class of Person, *John Osborn (who claimed that throughout his childhood no adult ever addressed a question to him) said that his grandmother, until the day she died when he was thirty, never once asked him anything about himself.*

Gradually the young learn to cope with small talk, and nourish the hope that sometimes it may grow into bigger talk. They outgrow the childhood level of exchange: "Where are you going?" "Out." "What are you going to do?" "Nothing." Unfortunately, however, there may be times when their coping will have to extend well beyond conversation.

The author of "The Coming of Age" is not one person but two: Jane Mayer and Clara Spiegel, who were classmates at Vassar.

THE headwaitress ushered the two middle-aged couples and the young girl into the deserted solarium. "We serve all our meals in here, now that it's so late in the season," she said.

They looked around and felt the desolateness of this sunroom, empty under the glaring, artificial light. The unset, yellow-painted tables and all the unoccupied straight-backed, yellow-painted chairs looked stiff and un-friendly; the blue-tiled floor shone hard and garish. Beyond the many windows the California night hid the gardens and pressed against the uncurtained panes to reflect the five people in grotesque distortion, swelling, too, the hanging shapes of the Japanese lanterns above them.

The room's cold simulation of warmth struck the party momentarily silent. Then Mrs. Ferguson, serene with the acceptance learned in her fifty years, spoke from the head of the small refectory table where they had just been seated.

"I'm really sorry about the main dining room being closed. I didn't realize they'd put us in the tearoom. I've never seen it without the sun before."

"Never mind," Mrs. Harris reassured her hostess com-fortably. She looked across the table at her husband to in-clude him in what she was saying. "What matters to Milton and me is that we're having this reunion with you and Lewis after fifteen years. And that we're finally meeting Sue. But I'm afraid it isn't very exciting here for you, Sue, is it, dear?"

Sue sickened at the patronizing tone and gave a polite smile, feeling no politeness. Everybody took her for eigh-teen, but it seemed as if her parents and their friends would never concede that she had grown up. There was Mrs. Har-ris' tone, for instance; but she could hardly be blamed after Sue's mother had said a minute ago, "Oh yes, Sue is nearly sixteen now...going on ninety, you know." Did it make them feel younger than their fifty-odd years, Sue wondered, to keep insisting that she was only fifteen? And

that only fifteen meant a little girl in every way? All her
mother's women friends treated her in that pat-the-little-
girl-on-the-head manner. The men weren't so bad now,
though. Most of them showed her a kind of mock exag-
gerated courtesy, as if they at least acknowledged her
young womanhood. They were all that way, she thought
with resignation, except this Mr. Harris sitting next to her.
She had only known him a half-hour. But she didn't like
him. He hadn't treated her like a baby, certainly, but there
was something else there, something that did not belong in
the face of her father's friends.

She let their conversation drift over her head. "Sorry it's
so empty here." "Late in the season." "Milton, you *must*
see the murals in the peacock room before we leave this
evening." The quiet, familiar tones of her mother's voice,
Mrs. Harris' Southern accent, the men's deeper tones.

Suddenly Mrs. Harris addressed her. "I used to know
your mother when she was your age."

Sue tried to look brightly interested.

"But she wasn't as pretty as you are," Mr. Harris
rumbled beside her.

Sue felt the intense, pathetic gratification of youth at
last accepted by its elders. She looked up at Mr. Harris
with a quick smile. Then she snatched her eyes away from
his. What a funny way for him to look at me, she thought.
She glanced quickly at her mother, but Mrs. Ferguson
hadn't seemed to notice anything. Her gray head was bent
toward Mrs. Harris', as they talked softly, reminiscing.

Sue ate her soup silently, her mind filled with thoughts
that were more emotion than words. She was an only child,
born to her parents late in their lives. She wanted so much
to be accepted into their adulthood, not pushed back any
more into that intermediate span of teens from which she
was certain she was ready to emerge.

Over her elders' conversation she heard a car drive up outside and her imagination peopled it at once with some people from Hollywood, a movie director and his wife. They would come to the door of this lighted room and see her sitting there, looking so young yet so composed among these older people. The director would see her, slim and small beside the huge Mr. Harris, and his practiced eyes would take in the shape of her face and the thick shoulder-length black hair which her father teasingly called her "glamour locks."

Look the director would say to his wife, that girl there, a type, what we've been looking for.

Unconsciously Sue straightened, sitting young and eager, her eyes on the door, her shoulders back, the beige wool of her light frock straining across her high young breasts.

Something insinuated into her daydream, became solid, real, sickening. Mr. Harris' leg, his knee was pressing against hers under the table. She looked up at him startled, but he was talking to her father, seemingly unaware of what he was doing. He couldn't have done it on purpose, she thought in shocked repudiation of her own suspicion. But then as she continued to stare at him she saw him clearly, awfully, in one complete instinct illuminated look. She saw his bigness, his heaviness, his grossness. There were bags of dark flesh beneath his eyes, and his cheeks were loose with the looseness of past dissipation. It was a face of jowls and pouches and thick drooping, sensuous lips. She saw his hands on the table, and they were horrible to her, immense hands with fleshy, freckled, hairy backs.

She shrank, drawing into herself, pressing her thighs tight together, moving all of herself beyound his disgusting touch.

"I'm afraid this empty place isn't very exciting for you

after all, Sue,'' Mrs. Ferguson said.

Oh, thank you, Mother, thank you for talking to me now. She smiled. "Oh, but it's fun, Mother, being out with you.'' Her eyes sought Mrs. Ferguson's, trying to convey to her what had happened, asking for help. But Mrs. Ferguson only smiled back encouragingly. As if she were helping me at a school play, Sue thought desparingly. She doesn't understand what I mean. She thinks I'm just flustered at being with grownups. Oh, Mother, don't let that man touch me again.

Imperceptibly she edged her chair closer to her father's, away from Mr. Harris. Now he couldn't touch her even when he leaned toward her to speak to her father.

She listened to her mother and Mrs. Harris talking of old mutual friends. She interjected remarks with false brightness. "You can't mean Mrs. Montgomery, Mother! She *never* could have been beautiful.''

"Oh, but she was, Sue, wasn't she, Eleanor? One of the prettiest girls at school.'' Mrs. Ferguson beamed on her daughter, showing her pleasure that Sue was able to enter into the conversation and still remember her place as a youngster.

Enveloped in that smile of her mother's and included now in the women's conversation, Sue began to feel safer, easier. It didn't matter that she had no interest in their friends, those indescribably dull and unromantic ladies who she was sure had never stirred or even wanted to stir sentimental desires in any boy's heart. She didn't want to think of romance now or love or anything like it. She wanted to feel protected. And they were safe, these ladies who were mother's friends, safe and comfortable and unalarming.

Then Mr. Harris suddenly spoke to her and in his tone

she sensed again that something which was like the slow pressure of his leg. His words were paternal enough, full of interest in the activities of youth, but the thing was there in his voice. She answered carefully, politely, aware of her father's attention, aware also, from the kindly expression of his face, that he did not understand what this man was doing to his daughter—for Mr. Harris was keeping her in the conversation, making her the center of it, holding her up to the others, holding her up for his own eyes.

She struggled to retain her composure, not to feel his looking at her. But it was there, a looking down, slantwise, so that as he appeared to bend a kindly paternal glance on her she could feel the finger tips of his eyes on her breasts, on her half-bare arms, her lap, and her thighs—his lids drooping, his lips drooping.

She looked up at her father, her eyes desperate. And she saw he had not noticed. Her mother, then? No, she did not see either. But his wife, Sue thought in an agony of shame, she must see. She must see and be sick and humiliated. But Mrs. Harris was nodding and smiling. They were all blind-folded with the complacence of their grown-upness. None of them could do any wrong. They could not see, because they would not see. And so they were letting Mr. Harris undress her with his eyes, feel her with his eyes, while they looked on smiling and approving.

A slow, sulky anger grew in Sue, a heat and at the same time a coldness, a scorn for her elders which was stronger than anything she had ever felt. How can they be so dumb, so unwilling to see? she thought. How can they be taken in by his idiotic fatherly business? He's disgusting, he's vile; I could throw up.

She grew hard now in her anger, sullen and unrespon-sive, furious at her elders who were permitting this to be done to her. She did not even hear how the conversation about the peacock room began.

"But you must see it, Milton," her mother was urging Mr. Harris. "It's a room for small dinners and the murals are really exquisite. It's a beautiful room."

"By all means, have a look at it," Mr. Ferguson said. "Go down to the end of the dining room off the lobby over there. It's the small room that opens off the end."

"You really shouldn't miss it," Mrs. Harris said. "I told you so after I was here yesterday."

"Oh, I want to see those paintings, all right," Mr. Harris said. "But I won't wait until after dinner. I'll go now." He pushed back his chair. "Will you be my guide, Sue?" He asked.

The girl's mind walked down the long, unlighted, narrow dining room to the small muraled room at the end, to the room in darkness with unknown light switches, to being there with this man.

"No," she said sullenly. "I won't be your guide."

There was a second's shocked, incredulous silence. The adults stared at her. She glared back stonily.

Then her mother said, "She doesn't mean that, do you, Sue?" There was warning and command in her tone.

And her father said in a voice of controlled quiet, "Of course, Milton, Sue will be glad to show you."

But they mustn't do this to me, they must not, Sue thought wildly. They must see what he wants, they must. They have to believe me. Are all grownups like that? They stick together. They won't help me; even my own father won't help me. Oh, please won't you have some faith in me, some faith in what I feel about this man?

She heard the polite patter with which her mother and Mrs. Harris were trying to cover up her sullen refusal. She heard Mr. Harris' laughter and joking with its my-my-what-a-naughty-girl overtone and she heard her father's order to show Mr. Harris the way to the peacock room. And so, abandoned, she gave in.

"All right," she said ungraciously. She got up and marched out of the room without looking back.

The dining room was long, dimly lighted for a few yards near the lobby, narrowing into total darkness at the far end where it opened into the black square of the unlighted peacock room. Sue's fear walked beside her down the center aisle between the ever-fading silhouettes of empty square tables set around with empty painted chairs. She felt how small she was and how thin and young. She felt the hugeness of the man lumbering behind her; she could hear his breathing and her flesh crept.

At the entrance to the peacock room she paused, feeling along the wall for a light switch, hastily, nervously. She felt him crowding toward her, pushing her into the room. She slid along the wall, her back to its surface, her outstretched hands searching frantically for a switch to release her with light. She could see nothing other than his face, hung, a dim pale patch above her, chin level with the top of her head.

She felt the suffocation of his suit closing her in between him and the wall, the rough dark wool against her, the smooth wall at her back. Then the immense hands descended on her, fumbling over her. "That's not the wall," she said, "that's me." She tried to move, to create a pretense that he, too, was looking for a light switch.

"That's you," he said thickly, "you, you. I want you. I want to kiss you." His breathing was loud, a thing which only her instinct understood. His hands were a horror.

She wanted to scream but couldn't. Then she knew with

sudden clarity that he was counting on her fear to keep her quiet, to keep her from struggling so that nothing could be seen when they rejoined the others, nothing to give either of them away.

And with this knowledge her fear was pushed out by anger that he should try to make her a conspirator against herself. It was a cold, strong anger, which was new to her experience, an anger which told her she was all-powerful here, that her intelligence was working, where he was beyond intelligence.

As his face came closer to her she pushed her doubled fists with all her strength against his chest. He stepped back from her, then groped forward again, his hands still too wanting for him to think of pinioning her arms.

"You. You." He kept repeating. "Don't do that to me. You're so exciting. I want you. You. You. I want to kiss you."

"Don't touch me again," she said quietly.

She felt his hands fumble out to her, his wet lips on her face. She struck him, slapping him hard across the cheek. The sound was sharp in the empty room.

The man stepped back.

She turned and felt her way to the door. She walked out down the funnel of the long dining room to its lighted end. She walked quietly. She did not touch her disarranged hair or stop to close the zipper of her dress where he had pulled it open half down the front. She knew her cheeks were white and her eyes blazing. She could still feel the muscles of her face pulling tight, at her lips, at her nostrils, at her lids.

She walked into the sunroom and quietly took her place at the table. For an instant no one noticed her. Then her mother said, "But Sue, what did you do with Mr. Harris? Where is—" The sentence died incomplete.

Sue saw the three pairs of incredulous adult eyes fixed on her. She felt hard and strong, sure of herself. This is what they deserve, she thought. This is what they deserve for their conspiracy to treat me like a child. This is their punishment for not believing me. Now they can see that I knew what I was doing.

I'm sorry for you, you fool, she thought, looking at Mrs. Harris and seeing the woman's weak blue eyes fill with tears. You ought to know what he's like. If you don't, look at him. Here he comes.

Mr. Harris walked in and took his seat. "Very interesting, those peacocks," he said. "Very beautiful."

In spite of his bent head the mark of Sue's slap was clear on his cheek.

"Oh," she said, hard and quiet, "so you saw them after all. Were you able to find the light switch after I left? You can see," she said to the others, "how he mistook me for the light switch."

She heard the gasp from her elders. She smiled an angry adult smile and turned to her mother.

"Could I have some coffee, please?" she asked.

She saw her mother's mind form the usual automatic "You know you're not allowed to drink coffee. You're too young yet." But the words were not spoken.

"Bring my daughter some coffee, please," Mrs. Ferguson said to the waitress.

LET GOD WORRY A LITTLE BIT
by Gertrude Berg

Throughout the Thirties and Forties hundreds of thousands of Americans listened to their Philcos and learned what Jewish family life could be like. The radio program was "The Goldbergs" and Gertrude Berg as Molly Goldberg played the Jewish mother who gently (and pungently) dominated the family, calming strife, uniting ememies, and in general, running things. She also wrote the scripts.

The scripts played an important part in helping to destroy what had been in America, as well as elsewhere, an unfortunate caricatured image of Jewish life. They also came at a time when, in another part of the world, Adolph Hitler was unleashing upon Jews furies the likes of which they had never known even as an historically persecuted people.

Gertrude Berg was born in upper Manhattan and her Yiddish accent was not natural to her. She explained that "My sense of Jewishness comes not from my father and mother so much as from my grandparents. We scarcely spoke Yiddish at home."

She drew her characters, however, from real life. When, in 1949, "The Goldbergs" became a television program there were installments about vacations at Pincus Pines, the family's real-life summer resort.

Gertrude Berg's relationship with God was wryly intimate; she never lost her confidence in Him. Were she alive today she would identify with Ann Landers when she wrote "I believe in a good God. . . . I think He is loving and all-protecting because He has loved and protected me. . . . I

talk to Him all the time, like Tevye in Fiddler on the Roof.
*I call God up like I call anybody up, and His line is never
busy."*

"MONEY," my father used to say, "is of no conse-
quence unless you owe it."

It was a point of honor with him to pay all debts when
due. But, beyond that, Jake Edelstein was most casual
about money. If an investment collapsed, as it frequently
did, he'd say to Mother, "Dinah, it was money we never
had." When a real pinch came, and our household fund
had to be commandeered for a creditor, Father would feel
slightly sheepish. "Let God worry about us a little bit," he
would say. Then he'd be off on his next business venture.

Over the years God must have worried a good deal. And
the year I was 15 I shared His concern.

For several summers, Father had run Fleischmann's
Hotel in the Catskill Mountains, near the village of Grif-
fins Corners. It was a shoestring operation. Each season he
opened by the grace of the local butcher, baker and hard-
ware merchant; each Labor Day he paid off his debts.
Then, consigning our worries to God, he would take us
back to our New York flat and would work through the
winter, managing a restaurant and saving toward another
summer.

We loved the hotel; when, that spring, Father revealed
that he just didn't have enough money to open it, I was
crushed. But, being 15 and sure of myself, I decided to

take matters into my own hands, I went secretly to my grandfather.

Mordecai Edelstein had come to America as an immigrant tinsmith with a talent for hard work. After a lifetime of labor, he had retired from his sheet-metal business in New Jersey, a well-to-do and respected citizen. But the pride and independence that had made him what he was were matched in his son Jake, and as a result the two of them didn't get on well. The last man in the world Jake would have approached for a loan was his father.

"Grandfather," I said, "I've worked hard at the hotel every summer, and I think I should be a partner. Would you lend me the money to buy a partnership from Papa?"

Mordecai pulled at his white handlebar mustache. He understood the maneuver at once, and he knew that his son was ignorant of it. "So how much do you need?" he asked.

"Five thousand dollars."

"All right, but"—and he shook a bony finger under my nose—"remember *you're* the partner, not me."

When I presented the proposition to Father, he realized that my $5,000 could have come only from Grandfather. But, so long as I didn't tell him, he could accept it, and that summer I endured for the first time the burden of debt. Every time a guest checked in, my heart was full of hope; every time one checked out I was in despair. All I could think of was the money I owed.

We had learned from experience that August 21 was the day when the hotel would begin to go into the black—if it was to go at all. The number of guests we retained from then until Labor Day made the summer worthwhile or a failure, and from this day forward rain and boredom were our mortal enemies. They could empty the hotel like a plague.

On August 21 I awoke at dawn to hear horrible splashing on the roof. I ran to Father's room and cried out in a choking whisper, "It's raining!" Father nodded grimly and headed toward the kitchen.

"Everybody look pleasant!" he commanded the assembled waiters and bus boys. A glazed smile was set on each countenance as it went out to face the breakfast guests. But the guests failed to respond. It was raining, and they took it as a personal affront from the management.

After breakfast they all filed out to the veranda to sit in the rocking chairs and look at the sky. It remained gray and wet. Luncheon was more dolorous than breakfast. After lunch they returned to the rockers and the rain. The last train for New York left at four o'clock, and I knew that the moment the first woman announced her departure the exodus would begin.

I also knew who would be first to make the move—a Mrs. Goldenson, whose boredom threshold was low. I kept my eyes on her. What I would do I wasn't sure. I couldn't tie her to the rocker, but something heroic would be demanded.

At 3:15, exactly time to pack and get to the station, Mrs. Goldenson sighed and stood up.

"Mrs. Goldenson!" I almost screamed from the far end of the porch. "How would you like your palm read, your fortune told?"

I was aghast to hear those words coming out of my mouth. I didn't know the first thing about palmistry.

Mrs. Goldenson hesitated. "Fortunes you tell?"

I whipped out a large handkerchief and tied it around my head. I bent over like an old woman and put a crack in my voice. "We gypsies know the future," I cackled.

Mrs. Goldenson smiled and winked at the others, but she sat down and extended her hand. The others crowded around. For a moment I studied her palm, and suddenly I *did* see her future.

All that summer, from my favorite reading spot—a big lobby chair by a window that opened on the porch—I had overheard the gossip and confidences exchanged by the ladies while they rocked. I had stored up everything I heard, and now it was my salvation.

Bending over Mrs. Goldenson's hand, I murmured, "You are a fortunate woman. You have the love of two men."

"Ah?" breathed the circle of kibitzers, pressing closer.

"One is rather short, middle-aged. I think he is bald...."

"Herman," she said with pleased possessiveness.

"The other is young and tall and handsome."

"Stanley, my son," she announced to the ladies.

"I see the two of them close together...I think in an office...."

"Supreme Fashions," she said.

"I see a cloud coming between you and your son Stanley."

"Never! What kind of a cloud?"

"It's not clear. Perhaps...another woman. Yes, a woman. She's in the same office with your husband and son."

"Eunice Meyers!" cried Mrs. Goldenson, striking her forehead with the palm of the hand I was trying to read. "I told Herman not to hire that girl!"

"I see a wedding," I said.

"I'll die!" she wailed. Then she stood up and said, "I have to telephone New York."

A few minutes later she returned to the porch. "Miss Edelstein, please make another room available. My husband and my son Stanley will be coming up this week-end."

Grandfather's money was safe for another 24 hours! The following morning the blessed sun shone.

Day by day I watched the ledger figures creep toward the black until our sole debt was the one that weighed most heavily upon me: Grandfather's loan. What if it rained again? I couldn't count on fortune-telling a second time. Then came another inspiration.

At dinner one evening I announced the production of a children's play, with auditions the next morning. I sat up that night to write the play—a mixture of Cinderella, Robin Hood, and Little Women. My problem was one not of art but of numbers. Our guests were 50-percent women, 40-pecent children and 10-percent week-end commuting husbands. I hoped to tie down as many children as possible.

The auditions were successful beyond my wildest hopes. Every child in the hotel appeared, some voluntarily, some prodded—and suddenly I had a cast of 35. Rehearsals were started, and after a week the parents began to demand a performance. I explained that more rehearsals would be necessary. A Mrs. Lowen wasn't satisfied. "Why can't we have the play tomorrow?" she asked.

"The actors aren't ready," I explained. "We need at least another week."

"I'm not expecting to stay so long. Maybe I'll have to take Patty out of the play."

Mrs. Lowen made a wry face. Patty was a spoiled brat, and we both knew that she'd scream bloody murder if Mrs. Lowen attempted such a thing.

At last I set the date for the performance: Labor Day, the last day of the hotel season. And I suggested that it would be nice for the cast to invite their uncles and aunts and cousins to come for the week-end.

I think the play went off reasonably well. After the performance, however, I came face to face with Mrs. Lowen. "Ten days I stayed over so Patty could be an actress," she said. "And what does Patty have to say? One speech, six words—I counted them. That's less than a word a day!"

"Patty had to serve an apprenticeship," I said. "Next year she'll have one of the leads."

"Yoweeee!" Patty exulted.

The morning after Labor Day, Father and I sat together in the tiny office while I ran up the figures on the adding machine. My hand trembled slightly as the total mounted. The final figure was $5367.92.

"We made it!" I cried.

I felt wonderfully free, and when Father pointed out that we would be practically broke after I had added interest to the loan, I said happily, "Let God worry about us a little bit."

Father laughed and threw his arms around me.

CONFESSIONS
by St. Augustine

Possibly the most famous "confession" book is The Confessions of Saint Augustine, *a classic of Christian mysticism. It has three aspects: a confession of sin, a confession of faith, a confession of praise. The book is also one of the many reasons why Augustine was recognized as a Doctor of the Church (a very small band), and it undoubtedly helped him to become Bishop of Hippo.*

Augustine was born into an African family of limited means, in Tagaste. His mother was a devout Christian, his father a liberal pagan. Because Augustine was very bright he was sent at the age of twelve or thirteen to the University of Madauros. Then in 370 he went to Carthage to continue his education. He was not only bright but sympathetic, charming, a shrewd observer of human nature and with an unusual capacity for friendship. In spite of these endearing qualities he became estranged from his family for a number of years.

Eventually they were reconciled and he was baptized in the Catholic Church on Easter Sunday, 387. He said to his mother, St. Monica, "I know and can confirm without the slightest hesitation, Mother, that it is through your prayers that God has given me the thought of putting above all else the discovery of truth, of wishing, meditating, loving nothing besides. And I strongly believe that it is your prayer which will enable me to acquire this most wonderful good which your own merits have made me desire."

ARRIVED now at adolescence I burned for all the satisfactions of hell, and I sank to the animal in a succession of dark lusts: *my beauty consumed away*, and I stank in Thine eyes, yet was pleasing in my own and anxious to please the eyes of men.

My one delight was to love and to be loved. But in this I did not keep the measure of mind to mind, which is the luminous line of friendship; but from the muddy concupiscence of the flesh and the hot imagination of puberty mists steamed up to becloud and darken my heart so that I could not distinguish the white light of love from the fog of lust. Both love and lust boiled within me, and swept my youthful immaturity over the precipice of evil desires to leave me half drowned in a whirlpool of abominable sins. Your wrath had grown mighty against me and I knew it not. I had grown deaf from the clanking of the chain of my mortality, the punishment for the pride of my soul: and I departed further from You, and You left me to myself: and I was tossed about and wasted and poured out and boiling over in my fornications: and you were silent, O my late-won Joy. You were silent, and I, arrogant and depressed, weary and restless, wandered further and further from You into more and more sins which could bear no fruit save sorrows.

If only there had been some one then to bring relief to the wretchedness of my state, and turn to account the fleeting beauties of these new temptations and bring within bounds their attractions for me: so that the tides of my youth might have driven in upon the shore of marriage: for then they might have been brought to calm with the having of children as Your law prescribes, O Lord, for in this way You form the offspring of this our death, able with gentle hand to blunt the thorns that You would not have in Your paradise. For Your omnipotence is not far from us, even when we are far from You. Or, on the other hand, I might well have listened more heedfully to the voice from the clouds: *Nevertheless such [as marry] shall have tribulation of the flesh; but I spare you"; and "It is good for a man not to touch a woman"; and "He that is without a wife is solicitous for the things that belong to the Lord, how he may please God: but he that is with a wife is solicitous for the things of the world, how he may please his wife."* I should have listened more closely to these words and made myself a eunuch for the kingdom of heaven; and so in all tranquility awaited Your embraces. Instead I foamed in my wickedness, following the rushing of my own tide, leaving You and going beyond all Your laws. Nor did I escape Your scourges. No mortal can. You were always by me, mercifully hard upon me, and besprinkling all my illicit pleasures with certain elements of bitterness, to draw me on to seek for pleasures in which no bitterness should be. And where was I to find such pleasures save in You O Lord, You who use sorrow to teach, and would us to heal, and kill us lest we die to You. Where then was I, and how far from the delights of Your house, in that sixteenth year of my life in this world, when the madness of lust—needing no licence from human shamelessness, receiving no licence from Your laws—took complete control of me, and I surrendered wholly to it? My family took no care to save me from this moral destruction by marriage: their only concern was that I should learn to make as fine and persuasive speeches as possible.

In that year my studies were interrupted. I had come back from Madaura, a neighbouring city to which I had been sent to study grammar and rhetoric, and the money was being got together for the longer journey to Carthage, where I was to go because my father was set up upon it—not that he was rich, for he was only a poor citizen of Tagaste. But to whom am I telling this? Not to Thee, O My God, but in Thy presence I am telling it to my own kind, to the race of men, or rather to that small part of the human race that may come upon these writings. And to what purpose do I tell it? Simply that I and any other who may read may realise out of what depths we must cry to Thee. For nothing is more surely heard by Thee than a heart that confesses Thee and a life in Thy faith.

Everyone of course praised my father because, although his means did not allow it, he had somehow provided the wherewithal for his son to travel so far for the sake of his studies. Many a very much richer citizen did no such thing for his children. Yet this same father never bothered about how I was growing towards You or how chaste or unchaste I might be, so long as I grew in eloquence, however much I might lack of Your cultivation O God, who are the one true and good Lord of Your field, my heart.

But during that sixteenth year between Madaura and Carthage, owing to the narrowness of the family fortunes I did not go to school, but I lived idly at home with my parents. The briars of unclean lusts grew so that they towered over my head, and there was no hand to root them out. On the contrary my father saw me one day in the public baths, now obviously growing towards manhood and showing the turbulent signs of adolescence. The effect upon him was that he already began to look forward to grandchildren, and went home in happy excitement to tell my mother. He rejoiced, indeed, through that intoxication in which the world forgets You its Creator and loves what You have created instead of You, the intoxication of the invisible wine of a will perverted and turned towards baseness. But in my mother's breast You had already laid the foundation of Your temple and begun Your holy habitation: whereas my father was still only a catechumen, and a new catechumen at that. So that she was stricken with a holy fear. And though I was not as yet baptised, she was in terror of my walking in the crooked ways of those who walk with their backs towards You and not their faces.

I have dared to say that You were silent, my God, when I went afar from You. But was it truly so? Whose but Yours were the words You dinned into my ears through the voice of my mother, Your faithful servant? Not that at that time any of it sank into my heart to make me do it. I still remember her anxiety and how earnestly she urged upon me not to sin with women, above all not with any man's wife. All this sounded to me womanish and I should have blushed to obey. Yet it was from You, though I did not know it and thought that You were silent and she speaking: whereas You were speaking to me through her, and in ignoring her I was ignoring You: I, her son, the son of Your handmaid, Your servant. But I realised none of this and went headlong on my course, so blinded that I was ashamed among the other youths that my viciousness was less than theirs; I heard them boasting of their exploits, and the viler the exploits the louder the boasting; and I set about the same exploits not only for the pleasure of the act but for the pleasure of the boasting.

Nothing is utterly condemnable save vice: yet I grew in vice through desire of praise; and when I lacked opportunity to equal others in vice, I invented things I had not done, lest I might be held cowardly for being innocent, or contemptible for being chaste. With the basest companions I walked the streets of Babylon [the city of this World as opposed to the city of God] and wallowed in its filth as if it had been a bed of spices and precious ointments. To make me cleave closer to that city's very center, the invisible Enemy trod me down and seduced me, for I was easy to seduce. My mother had by now fled out of the center of Babylon, but she still lingered in its outskirts. She had urged me to chastity but she did not follow up what my father had told her of me: and though she saw my sexual passions as most evil now and full of peril for the future, she did not consider that if they could not be pared down to the quick, they had better be brought under control within the bounds of married love. She did not want me married because she feared that a wife might be a hindrance to my prospects—not those hopes of the world to come which my mother had in You, O God, but my prospects as a student. Both my parents were unduly set upon the success of my studies, my father because he had practically no thought of You and only vain ambition for me, my mother because she thought that the usual course of studies would be not only no hindrance to my coming to You but an actual help. Recalling the past as well as I can, that is how I read my parents' characters. Anyhow, I was left to do pretty well as I liked, and go after pleasure not only beyond the limit of reasonable discipline but to sheer dissoluteness in many kinds of evil. And in all this, O God, a mist hung between my eyes and the brightness of Your truth: *and mine iniquity had come forth as it were from fatness.*

Your law, O Lord, punishes theft; and this law is so written in the hearts of men that not even the breaking of it blots it out: for no thief bears calmly being stolen from—not even if he is rich and the other steals through want. Yet I chose to steal, and not because want drove me to it—unless a want of justice and contempt for it and an excess for iniquity. For I stole things which I already had in plenty and of better quality. Nor had I any desire to enjoy the things I stole, but only the stealing of them and the sin. There was a pear tree near our vineyard, heavy with fruit, but fruit that was not particularly tempting either to look at or to taste. A group of young blackguards, and I among them, went out to knock down the pears and carry them off late one night, for it was our bad habit to carry on our games in the streets till very late. We carried off an immense load of pears, not to eat—for we barely tasted them before throwing them to the hogs. Our only pleasure in doing it was that it was forbidden. Such was my heart, O God, such was my heart: yet in the depth of the abyss You had pity on it. Let that heart now tell You what it sought when I was thus evil for no object, having no cause for wrongdoing save my wrongness. The malice of the act was base and I loved it—that is to say I loved my own undoing, I loved the evil in me—not the thing for which I did the evil, simply the evil: my soul was depraved, and hurled itself down from security in You into utter destruction, seeking no profit from wickedness but only to be wicked.

INGRID BERGMAN—MY STORY
by Ingrid Bergman and Alan Burgess

Gifted, poised, beautiful, and able to perform in several languages—this was the Ingrid Bergman whom world audiences would proclaim as one of the finest actresses of her time. As a child, however, her shyness was so intense that upon occasion it manifested itself in severe physical symptoms: swollen fingers too stiff to bend, swollen lips, swollen eyelids. But drama school ended all her illnesses.

She writes of her joy there: "I became a terribly happy person, out-going, relaxed, because I was doing exactly what I wanted to do. And it was so very easy for me." She took classes in ballet, fencing, voice projection, posture, and the history of the theatre. And she played scenes.

Such were her days. Nights, the students were permitted to see all the performances without cost from the top gallery.

After only three months at the Royal Dramatic School she was picked for an important part in a play, an unusual occurrence for a beginning student. Her delight was short-lived. Her being singled out produced so violent a reaction upon the part of her classmates that the Director of the Royal Dramatic Theatre said that she would have to leave the cast or he would have a house revolution.

In the following excerpt Ingrid Bergman tells of auditioning for admission to Stockholm's Royal Dramatic School.

THERE was a sense of urgency about the young girl in the tweed skirt, beige-colored sweater she had knitted herself, and common-sense walking shoes who hurried toward the bright open quayside of Stockholm's Strandvägen. Approaching eighteen, she was now beginning to fill out a bit. A year or so earlier, her Aunt Hulda's suggestion that she should wear three pairs of woolen stockings to pad out her calves had not added to her assurance; in her own words, she had been "the thinnest child ever."

She lacked security. She was terribly shy. She was frightened of people, and of the world generally. And at that moment she was extremely apprehensive. This was, without doubt, the most important morning of her life. If she muffed this opportunity, the world ended. She could forget her daydreams of vast audiences applauding as she made her tenth curtsy at the conclusion of a monumental opening night.

She had made her promise to Uncle Otto. If this attempt failed, she might become a salesperson or somebody's secretary, but those dreams of theatrical fame would stop. Uncle Otto was convinced that actresses were little different from prostitutes! "You can't tell me, young lady. I've seen those love scenes they do on the stage and in those films; you can't tell me they don't go on doing the same thing—*afterwards!*"

She wouldn't even attempt to argue with him. She knew that he was trying to fill in for her father, to see that she had a good education and was brought up properly. Her compulsive involvement with play-acting, the restless urge to go on the stage, distressed him enormously. As a staunch, if not punctilious Lutheran, he felt it was his duty to save her from a life of shame; as her guardian he owed that to her father's memory. But he knew that she was stubborn and determined; he knew that to dismiss this passionate dream of hers out of hand, not to give her even the opportunity, would leave her heartbroken and would not be fair. Therefore he had given her one chance.

"All right," he said. "You shall have the fees you need for the extra tuition. You can try for the Royal Dramatic School. Take the examinations—do whatever auditions you have to do. But if you fail, that's the end of it. Understand that. No more of this actress nonsense. And I want your promise, because I know you will keep that promise. Do you accept this?"

Accept it? She had leapt at it. Without professional training, for which she needed money—her own money it was true, left in trust to Uncle Otto by her father—her chances would be diminished. And as for failing, that was inconceivable. Beyond her comprehension. God could not have influenced her for all these years if he intended her to fail. Certainly she knew that there were seventy-five applicants this year and that only very few would be selected.

But if the judges had to choose only *one*, then she *had* to be that one. Otherwise life would be insupportable.

She paused in front of the massive, pale gray facade of the theater. Beyond stretched the waterfront, backed by the symmetrical curve of seven-story apartment buildings, shops and offices, surmounted by the domes of copper cupolas, tarnished to a pale sea-green by the salty winds blown in from the northern seas. She breathed in deeply. She belonged to this city of lakes and ferryboats and glittering water. She had been born no more than a hundred yards from this theater, in the apartment above her father's photographic shop along there on the Strandvägen.

She regarded the broad stone steps. Four impressive lamps, their bulbs round and opalescent as immense onions, dominated the entrance. On either side of the doors stood gilded statues of male and female figures, representing the Muses, including her beloved Thalia, Ingrid's goddess of the theater. She went around to the stage door and crossed to the office where the porter peered at the list of applicants to be auditioned that morning.

She went outside again, crossed the road to the small park against the quayside, stared straight in the eye of the giant, bearded, bronze head of John Ericsson, Swedish engineer and inventor of the first armored battleship, mentally rehearsed her opening line, made one or two tentative leaps to prepare for her magnificent entrance, wandered around a bit, looked at the passing seagulls, and returned to the theater still fifteen minutes before her time was due.

Some weeks previously she had delivered to the Royal Dramatic Theater her big brown envelope which contained the three pieces she had chose for her audition. The jury would select the two she was to perform. She was aware that she could be failed at either the first or second test. If she failed, the porter would give her back the big brown envelope, and that would be the end of her. But if she passed, she would get a smaller white envelope which would tell her the date of her next audition, and which of her audition pieces the jury wished to hear.

Ingrid had discussed her choice of material with Gabriel Alw, her drama teacher. "The first audition must be the most important," she said. "Practically everybody else will be doing heavy dramatic pieces, Camille or Lady Macbeth, wailing and weeping all over the stage. I think the jury will be so bored having to watch a procession of young girls breaking their hearts. Can't we make the jury laugh?"

Gabriel had agreed with her diagnosis. "Good idea. And I know a play by a Hungarian which would be just right. A peasant girl, pretty and gay, is teasing this bold country

boy who's trying to flirt with her. She's even bolder than
he is. She leaps across this small stream toward him.
Stands there, hands on her hips, laughing at him. How's
that for an entrance? You make a flying jump out of the
wings onto the stage, and you stand there, legs apart,
hands on hips, as if to say, "Here I am. Look at me! Are
you paying attention!"

* * *

So this was the play I work on. I wait in the wings and then
I'm called. You do the audition on the stage, all by
yourself. Any other dialogue is thrown at you from the
wings, in my case, by the boy who was playing the country
lad, who also acted as prompter if I dried up. So here I go.
A run and a leap into the air, and there I am in the middle
of the stage with that big gay laugh that's supposed to stop
them dead in their tracks. I pause, and get out my first line.
Then I take a quick glance down over the footlights at the
jury. And I can't believe it! They are paying not the
slightest attention to me. In fact the jury members in the
front row are chatting to the others in the second row. I
dry up in absolute horror. I simply can't remember the
next line. The boy throws the cue at me. I get that out. But
now the jury are talking in loud voices and gesticulating. I
go blank with despair. At least they could hear me out, let
me finish. I can't concentrate, can't remember anything. I
hiss to the boy, "What's my next line?" But before he can
say it, I hear the voice of the chairman of the jury: "Stop
it, stop it. That's enough. Thank you, thank you
miss...next please, next please."

I walk off stage. I don't see anybody or hear anything. I
walk out through the foyer. I walk out into the street. And

I'm thinking—Now I have to go home and face Uncle Otto. Now I have to tell him that I'm thrown off the stage after about thirty seconds. I have to say, "They didn't listen to me. They didn't even think I was worth listening to." Now I can't think of becoming an actress ever again. So life isn't worth living. I walk straight across to the quayside. And I know there's only one thing to do. Throw myself into the water and commit suicide.

* * *

She stood near the little kiosk where the ferry tickets to Djurgården and Skansen were sold. There was no one about; a few seagulls screaming in the distance, two or three floating on the surface. Far away across the water the graceful golden tower of the Nordiska Museum. The water was dark and shining. She took a step closer and peered at it. It *was* dark and shining...and *dirty*. She would be covered with dirt when they pulled her out. Not like Ophelia floating beneath the crystal-clear, lily fragrant stream in Shakespeare's Arden Arcadia. She'd have to swallow that stuff. Ugh! That was no good.

Temporarily, suicide was set aside. But still in despair she turned on her heel and began the uphill walk through the shops and main streets up to the apartment block where she lived. The long slender legs had no animation now. In the apartment her two girl cousins were waiting for her. They were the last people she wanted to see. Oh, for the comfort of her room where she could throw herself on the bed and weep and weep and weep and weep . . . . If only Mama or Papa were alive and could comfort her. Why did they have to die so soon? And now Britt and Margit just wouldn't leave her alone. "What's

taken you so long?'' ''Yes, where've you been?'' Stupid
questions. How could she tell these two horrible, grinning
girls that by now, if the water hadn't been so dirty, she'd
be a romantic corpse floating out to sea?

''Lars Seligman has been on the phone . . . . '' Lars?
What could he want? They were close friends, he also trying to pass his auditions. ''He said he'd been down to the
office to collect his white envelope. . . . And he asked
what sort of envelope you'd got . . . . And *they said you
got a white envelope too . . . .*''

A white envelope? She'd got a white envelope? Could
they be telling the truth? There was no time for discussion.
She turned and ran. She raced down the stairs, she ran into
the street. It was downhill all the way, but she would swear
her feet never touched the ground until she reached the
theater. She arrived at the office as if blown in by a storm
wind. ''What sort of envelope have I got? Please tell me
what sort of envelope I've got?'' The porter smiled: ''A
white one, Miss Bergman . . . we wondered where you'd
been. Here it is. Good luck . . . . ''

She tore it open. ''Your next audition will be . . . . ''
She couldn't read the date, but she read that they would
like her to audition with the piece she had chosen from
Rostand's *L'Aiglon*. She floated out in the sweet summer
air. Oh, how wonderful life was, oh, how lucky she was to
have Britt, and Uncle Otto, and Aunt Hulda, and wasn't
Stockholm the most beautiful city in the whole wide world,
and that dark and shining water stretching away to some
distant enchanted horizon was the most glorious thing she
had ever seen.

* * *

I was so happy to be accepted that I didn't bother to ask why they'd been so brusque and inattentive when I leapt onto the stage. It was not until many years later in Italy that I got the answer. I was in Rome and there was Alf Sjöberg who was one of the jury at the audition. And it all came back to me, and I said, "Tell me, please tell me, why at that first audition did you all treat me so badly? I could have committed suicide, you treated me so nastily, and disliked me so much." Alf stared at me as if I'd gone mad. "Disliked you so much! Dear girl, you're crazy! The minute you leapt out of the wings onto the stage, and stood there laughing at us, we turned round and said to each other, 'Well, we don't have to listen to her, she's in! Look at that security. Look at that stage presence. Look at that impertinence! You jumped out onto the stage like a tigress. You weren't afraid of us. 'No need to waste another second, we've got dozens more to look at. Next please.' So what are you talking about. You might never make as good an entrance in your life again.''

REUNION
by Fred Uhlman

"He came into my life in February 1932 and never left it again." With that line Fred Uhlman opens Reunion, *a story of friendship between Hans Schwarz and Graf Konradin von Hohenfels as told by the former. Hans goes on to say "I can remember the day and the hour when I first set eyes on this boy who was to be the source of my greatest happiness and my greatest despair. It was two days after my sixteenth birthday, at three o'clock in the afternoon on a grey, dark German winter's day. I was at the Karl Alexander Gymnasium in Stuttgart, Württemberg's most famous grammar school . . . ."*

Hans Schwarz was the son of a Jewish doctor, grandson and great-grandson of rabbis. Konradin von Hohenfels belonged to an illustrious Swabian family that was an important part of German history. Yet the two became friends because they wanted to be friends. This made it possible for them to transcend for a time class, religion, ideology, but the latter two in particular were to catch up with them and to cause the eventual end of their friendship.

When Hans' parents sent him to America (almost a year after he and Konradin had become friends) to spare him the torments of Hitler's Germany, Konradin wrote Hans how sad he was to have him leave. In that same letter he expressed his admiration for Hitler, and his belief that only he could save Germany from materialism and Bolshevism.

Thirty years later, by then a lawyer in America, Hans Schwarz received an appeal from the Karl Alexander Gymnasium asking him to subscribe to a war memorial for the

*boys who had fallen in the Second World War. He steeled
himself to look at the letter "H" and under it read:
VON HOHENFELS, Konradin, implicated in the
plot to kill Hitler.* Executed."

I CAN'T remember exactly when I decided that Konradin
had to be my friend, but that one day he *would* be my
friend I didn't doubt. Until his arrival I had been without a
friend. There wasn't one boy in class who I believed could
live up to my romantic ideal of friendship, not one whom I
really admired, for whom I would have been willing to die
and who could have understood my demand for complete
trust, loyalty and self-sacrifice. All of them struck me as
more or less clumsy, rather commonplace, healthy and
unimaginative Swabians—even the Caviar lot seemed no
exception. Most of the boys were pleasant and I got on well
enough with them. But just as I had no particularly strong
feeling for them, so they had none for me. I never visited
their homes and they never came to our house. Perhaps
another reason for my coolness was that they all appeared
to be so immensely practical, and already knew what they
wanted to be, lawyers, officers, teachers, pastors and
bankers. I alone had no idea, only vague dreams and even
vaguer desires. All I knew was that I wanted to travel, and
I believed that one day I would be a great poet.

* * *

All I knew, then, was that he was going to be my friend.
Everything attracted me to him. First and foremost the
glory of his name which singled him out—for me—from all
the other boys, including the 'vons' (just as I would have
been more attracted by the Duchesse de Guermantes than

by a Madame Meunier). Then his proud bearing, his manners, his elegance, his good looks—and who could be
altogether insensitive to them?—powerfully suggested to
me that here at last I had found someone who came up to
my ideal of a friend.

The problem was how to attract him to me. What could
I offer him, who had gently but firmly turned down the
aristocrats and the Caviar? How could I conquer him entrenched behind barriers of tradition, his natural pride and
acquired arrogance? Moreover he seemed quite content to
be alone and to stay aloof from the other boys, with whom
he mixed only because he had to.

How to attract his attention, how to impress him with
the fact that I was different from this dull crowd, how to
convince him that I alone ought to be his friend—this was
a problem for which I had no clear answer. All I knew in-
stinctively was that I had to *stand out*. Suddenly I began to
take a new interest in what was going on in class. Normally
I was happy to be left alone with my dreams, undisturbed
by question or problems, waiting for the bell to release me
from drudgery. There had been no particular reason why I
should impress my schoolmates. As long as I passed my
exams, which didn't give me much difficulty, why exert
myself? Why impress the teachers? Those tired, disillusioned old men who used to tell us that *non scholae sed vitae
discimus* when it seemed to me that it was the other way
round?

But now I came to life. I jumped up whenever I felt I had
anything to say. I discussed *Madame Bovary*, and the existence or non-existence of Homer, I attacked Schiller,
called Heine a poet for commercial travellers and made
Hölderlin out to be Germany's greatest poet, "even greater
than Goethe." Looking back I see how childish it all

was—yet I certainly electrified my teachers and even the Caviar took notice. The results also surprised me. The masters, who had given me up, suddenly felt that their efforts hadn't been wasted after all, and that at last they were getting some reward for their labour. They turned to me with renewed hope and a touching, almost pathetic joy. They asked me to translate and to explain scenes from *Faust* and *Hamlet*, which I did with real pleasure and, I like to believe, some understanding. My second determined effort came during the few hours dedicated to physical exercise. At that time—perhaps it's different today—our teachers at the Karl Alexander Gymnasium considered sport a luxury. To chase or hit a ball as was the habit in America and Britain seemed to them a terrible waste of valuable time which could be more beneficially devoted to acquiring knowledge. Two hours a week to strengthen one's body was regarded as adequate, if not more than enough. Our gym instructor was a noisy, tough little man, Max Loehr, known as Muscle Max, who was desperately keen on developing our chests and arms and legs as intensively as possible in the short time at his disposal. In this cause he employed three internationally notorious instruments of torture—the Horizontal Bar, the Parallel Bars and the Vaulting Horse. The usual form was a run round the hall, then some bending and stretching. After this warming-up Muscle Max would go to his favorite instrument of the three, the Horizontal Bar, and show us a few exercises, as easy for him as falling off a log, but for most of us extremely difficult. Usually he would ask one of the most agile boys to emulate his performance and sometimes he picked on me, but in the last months he had more often called on Eisemann, who loved showing off and anyway wanted to be a Reichswehr officer.

This time I was determined to get my oar in. Muscle Max went back to the Horizontal Bar, stood to attention under it, stretched up his arms and then jumped elegantly, grasping the rod in his iron grip. With incredible ease and skill he raised his body slowly inch by inch up to the bar until it rested there. Then he turned to the right, stretched both arms out, back to the old position, turned to the left, and back to rest. But suddenly he seemed to fall, for a moment he hung suspended by his knees, his hands almost touching the floor. Slowly he started swinging, faster and faster, till he was back at his place on the bar and then—with a quick, magnificent movement—he launched himself into the void and landed with the lightest of thuds on his toes. His expertise made the feat seem easy, though in fact it needed complete control, a wonderful balance and also nerve. Of the three qualities, I had something of the first two, but I can't say I was very brave. Often at the last moment I doubted if I could do it. I hardly dared let go, and when I did it never entered my head that I should do it nearly as well as Muscle Max. It was the difference between a juggler able to keep six balls in the air and somebody thankful to be able to manage three.

On this particular occasion I stepped forward as soon as Max had finished his demonstration and stared him straight in the eyes. He hesitated for a second, and then "Schwarz," he said.

I walked slowly to the bar, stood to attention and jumped. My body, like his, rested on the rod. I looked round. I saw Max below me, ready for any slip-up. The boys stood quiet and watched me. I looked at Hohenfels and when I saw his eyes focused on me I raised my body from right to left and from left to right, hung on my knees, swung upwards and rested for a second on the bar. I had no fear, only one will and one desire. I was going to do it for *him*. Suddenly I raised my body right up, jumped over the bar, flew in the air—and then *thump!*

At least I was on my feet.

There were some suppressed giggles, but a few of the boys clapped; they weren't such bad fellows, some of them . . . .

Standing quite still I looked at *him*. Needless to say Konradin hadn't giggled. He hadn't clapped either. But he looked at *me*.

A few days later, I came to school with a few Greek coins—I had been collecting coins since I was twelve. I brought a Corinthian silver drachma, an owl of Pallas Athene, a head of Alexander the Great, and as soon as he approached his place, I pretended to be studying them through a magnifying glass. He saw me looking at them and, as I had hoped, his curiosity got the better of his restraint. He asked me if he might look at them too. From the way he handled the coins I could see he knew something about them; he had the collector's way of fondling the beloved objects and the collector's appreciative caressing look. He told me he collected coins too, and that he had the owl but didn't have my head of Alexander. He also had some coins which I hadn't.

Here we were interrupted by the entrance of the teacher and by the ten o'clock interval. Konradin seemed to have lost interest and left the room without even looking at me. Still—I felt happy. It was the first time he had talked to me and I was determined it should not be the last.

* * *

Three days later, on March 15th—I shall always

remember the date—I was going home from school. It was
a soft, cool, spring evening. The almond trees were in full
bloom, the crocuses were out and the sky was pastel blue
and sea green, a Northern sky with a touch of Italy. I saw
Hohenfels in front of me and he seemed to hesitate and to
be waiting for somebody. I slowed down—I was afraid of
overtaking him—but I had to go on for it would have looked ridiculous not to, and he might have misunderstood my
hesitation. When I had almost reached him he turned and
smiled at me. Then, with a strangely gauche and still hesi-
tant movement, he shook my trembling hand. "Hello,
Hans," he said, and suddenly I realized to my joy and
relief and amazement that he was as shy and as much in
need of a friend as I.

I can't remember much of what Konradin said to me
that day or what I said to him. All I know is that we walked
up and down for an hour, like two young lovers, still nervous, still afraid of each other, but somehow I knew that
this was only a beginning and that from now on my life
would no longer be empty and dull, but full of hope and
richness for us both.

When at last I left him I ran all the way home. I laughed,
I talked to myself, I wanted to shout and sing and I found
it very difficult not to tell my parents how happy I was,
that my whole life had changed, and that I was no longer a
beggar but as rich as Croesus. Fortunately my parents were
too preoccupied to notice the change in me. They were
used to my moody and bored expressions, my evasive
answers and my prolonged silences which they attributed
to "growing pains" and the mysterious transition from
adolescence to manhood. Occasionally my mother had
tried to penetrate my defenses, once or twice she had tried
to stroke my hair, but she had given this up long ago,

discouraged by my stubbornness and lack of response.

But later a reaction set in. I slept badly, because I was afraid of the morning. Perhaps he had already forgotten me or regretted his surrender? Perhaps it had been a mistake to let him feel how much I needed his friendship! Should I have been more cautious, more reserved? Perhaps he had told his parents about me and they had warned him against chumming up with a Jew! So I went on torturing myself until at last I fell into a restless sleep.

* * *

But all my fears proved to be groundless. As soon as I went into the classroom Konradin came straight up and sat next to me. His pleasure at seeing me was so genuine, so unmistakable, that even I, with my inbred suspicions, lost all fear. It was clear to me from what he said that he had slept extremely well and that not for a moment had he doubted my sincerity, and I felt ashamed of ever having suspected him.

From this day on we were inseparable. We always left school together—our homes were in the same direction—and he waited for me in the mornings. The class, amazed to begin with, soon took our friendship for granted—except for Bollacher, who later nicknamed us "Castor and Pollack," and the Caviar, who decided to cut us.

The next few months were the happiest of my life. Spring came and the whole country was one mass of blossoms, cherry and apple, pear and peach while the poplars took on their silver and the willows their lemon yellow. The soft, serene bluish hills of Swabia were covered with vineyards and orchards and crowned with castles, and these small medieval towns had high gabled town halls, and from their fountains, standing on pillars and surrounded by water-spouting monsters, there looked down stiff, comic, heavily-armed and moustachioed Swabian dukes or counts with names like Eberhardt the Wellbeloved or Ulrich the Terrible; and the Neckar flowed gently round willowy isles. All of this conveyed a feeling of peace, of trust in the present and hope for the future.

THE FINDING IN THE TEMPLE
by St. Luke

For the ancient Jews the temple in Jerusalem was the dwelling place of the Lord. It played a central part throughout their lives. For instance, when a Jewish boy was twelve, he went to the temple to become bar mitzvah, "a son of the Law, able to accept for himself the responsibilities and obligations to which his parents had committed him by the rite of circumcision."

For Jesus this visit to the temple, his second, marks his entry into adulthood.

AND the child grew, and waxed strong in spirit, filled with wisdom: and the grace of God was upon him.

Now his parents went to Jerusalem every year at the feast of the passover.

And when he was twelve years old, they went up to Jerusalem, after the custom of the feast.

And when they had fulfilled the days, as they returned, the child Jesus tarried behind in Jerusalem; and Joseph and his mother knew not of it.

But they, supposing him to have been in the company, went a day's journey; and they sought him among their kinsfolk and acquaintance.

And when they found him not, they turned back again to Jerusalem, seeking him.

And it came to pass, that after three days they found him in the temple, sitting in the midst of the doctors, both hearing them, and asking them questions.

And all that heard him were astonished at his understanding and answers.

And when they saw him, they were amazed; and his mother said unto him, Son, why hast thou thus dealt with us? behold, thy father and I have sought thee sorrowing.

And he said unto them, How is it that ye sought me? wist ye not that I be about my Father's business?

And they understood not the saying which he spake unto them.

And he went down with them, and came to Nazareth, and was subject unto them: but his mother kept all these sayings in her heart.

And Jesus increased in wisdom and stature, and in favour with God and man.

BLACK BOY
by Richard Wright

Born on a Mississippi plantation in 1908, Richard Wright as a small child was often hungry, often drunk, often beaten. It was not just the White South that oppressed him growing up. He was oppressed within his own authoritarian and bigoted home where he found little warmth and tenderness.

Even worse, men frequenting the neighborhood saloon enticed him when he was five to drink whiskey to the point of intoxication. Soon he acquired the habit of begging drinks and became a child drunkard. In despair his mother beat him and prayed and wept over him. His craving for alcohol finally disappeared.

At a later age than usual Richard Wright entered school. His father had deserted the family and his mother, working as a cook, had found it difficult to afford the clothes necessary to make him presentable. Not until he was nine was he "able to read and count." Over the years his passion for reading was to be the strongest factor in his education.

By the time he was nearly seventeen and graduating from grammar school he had resolved firmly that he would resist every effort to mold him, whatever the source. His was the right to his own mind. After graduation he left home and went to Memphis. Eventually he quit the South for Chicago where he hoped his mother, now paralyzed, his aunt and his brother would join him. In the North he sought a life that could be lived with dignity.

There after many hardships he became a distinguished writer. In 1932 he joined the Communist Party, but later, disillusioned, left it. After World War II he lived and died in Paris.

THE school term ended. I was selected as valedictorian of my class and assigned to write a paper to be delivered at one of the public auditoriums. One morning the principal summoned me to his office.

"Well, Richard Wright, here's your speech," he said with smooth bluntness and shoved a stack of stapled sheets across his desk.

"What speech?" I asked as I picked up the papers.

"The speech you're to say the night of graduation," he said.

"But, professor, I've written my speech already," I said.

He laughed confidently, indulgently.

"Listen, boy, you're going to speak to both *white* and colored people that night. What can you alone think of saying to them? You have no experience . . . "

I burned.

"I know that I'm not educated, professor," I said. "But the people are coming to hear the students, and I won't make a speech that you've written."

He leaned back in his chair and looked at me in surprise.

"You know, we've never had a boy in this school like you before," he said. "You've had your way around here. Just how you managed to do it, I don't know. But, listen, take this speech and say it. I know what's best for you. You can't afford to just say *anything* before those white people that night." He paused and added meaningfully: "The superintendent of schools will be there; you're in a position to make a good impression on him. I've been a principal for more years than you are old, boy. I've seen many a boy and girl graduate from this school, and none of them was too proud to recite a speech I wrote for them."

I had to make up my mind quickly; I was faced with a matter of principle. I wanted to graduate, but I did not want to make a public speech that was not my own.

"Professor, I'm going to say my own speech that night," I said.

He grew angry.

"You're just a young, hotheaded fool," he said. He toyed with a pencil and looked up at me. "Suppose you don't graduate?"

"But I passed my examinations," I said.

"Look, mister," he shot at me. "I'm the man who says who passes at this school."

I was so astonished that my body jerked. I had gone to this school for two years and I had never suspected what kind of man the principal was; it simply had never occurred to me to wonder about him.

"Then I don't graduate," I said flatly.

I turned to leave.

"Say, you. Come here," he called.

I turned and faced him; he was smiling at me in a remote, superior sort of way.

"You know, I'm glad I talked to you," he said. "I was seriously thinking of placing you in the school system, teaching. But, now I don't think that you'll fit."

He was tempting me, baiting me; this was the technique that snared black young minds into supporting the southern way of life.

"Look professor, I may never get a chance to go to school again," I said. "But I like to do things right."

"What do you mean?"

"I've no money. I'm going to work. Now, this ninth-grade diploma isn't going to help me much in life. I'm not bitter about it; it's not your fault. But I'm just not going to do things this way."

"Have you talked to anybody about this?" he asked me.

"No, why?"

"Are you sure?"

"This is the first I've heard of it, professor," I said, amazed again.

"You haven't talked to any white people about this?"

"No, sir!"

"I just wanted to know," he said.

My amazement increased; the man was afraid now for his job!

"Professor, you don't understand me." I smiled.

"You're just a young, hot fool," he said, confident again. "Wake up, boy. Learn the world you're living in. You're smart and I know what you're after. I've kept closer track of you than you think. I know your relatives. Now, if you play safe," he smiled and winked, "I'll help you to go to school to college."

"I want to learn, professor," I told him. "But there are some things I don't want to know."

"Good-bye," he said.

I went home, hurt but determined. I had been talking to a "bought" man and he had tried to "buy" me. I felt that I had been dealing with something unclean. That night Griggs, a boy who had gone through many classes with me, came to the house.

"Look, Dick, you're throwing away your future here in Jackson," he said. "Go to the principal, talk to him, take his speech and say it. I'm saying the one he wrote. So why can't you? What the hell? What can you lose?"

"No," I said.

"Why?"

"I know only a hell of a little, but my speech is going to reflect that," I said.

"Then you're going to be blacklisted for teaching jobs," he said.

"Who the hell said I was going to teach?" I asked.

"God, but you've got a will," he said.

"It's not will. I just don't want to do things that way," I said.

He left. Two days later Uncle Tom came to me. I knew that the principal had called him in.

"I hear that the principal wants you to say a speech which you've rejected," he said.

"Yes, sir. That's right," I said.

"May I read the speech you've written?" he asked.

"Certainly," I said, giving him my manuscript.

"And may I see the one that the principal wrote?"

I gave him the principal's speech too. He went to his room and read them. I sat quiet, waiting. He returned.

"The principal's speech is the better speech," he said.

"I don't doubt it," I replied. "But why did they ask me to write a speech if I can't deliver it?"

"Would you let me work on your speech?" he asked.

"No, sir."

"Now, look, Richard, this is your future . . . "

"Uncle Tom, I don't care to discuss this with you," I said.

He stared at me, then left. The principal's speech was simpler and clearer than mine, but it did not say anything; mine was cloudy, but it said what I wanted to say. What could I do? I had half a mind not to show up at the graduation exercises. I was hating my environment more each day. As soon as school was over, I would get a job, save money, and leave.

Griggs, who had accepted a speech written by the principal, came to my house each day and we went off into the woods to practice orating; day in and day out we spoke to the trees, to the creeks, frightening the birds, making the cows in the pastures stare at us in fear. I memorized my speech so thoroughly that I could have recited it in my sleep.

The news of my clash with the principal had spread through the class and the students became openly critical of me.

"Richard, you're a fool. You're throwing away every chance you've got. If they had known the kind of fool boy you are, they would never have made you valedictorian," they said.

I gritted my teeth and kept my mouth shut, but my rage was mounting by the hour. My classmates, motivated by a desire to "save" me, pestered me until I all but reached the breaking point. In the end the principal had to caution them to let me alone, for fear I would throw up the sponge and walk out.

I had one more problem to settle before I could make my speech. I was the only boy in my class wearing short pants and I was grimly determined to leave school in long pants. Was I not going to work? Would I not be on my own? When my desire for long pants became known at home, yet another storm shook the house.

"You're trying to go too fast," my mother said.

"You're nothing but a child," Uncle Tom pronounced.

"He's beside himself," Granny said.

I served notice that I was making my own decisions from then on. I borrowed money from Mrs. Bibbs, my employer, made a down payment on a pearl-gray suit. If I could not pay for it, I would take the damn thing back after graduation.

On the night of graduation I was nervous and tense; I rose and faced the audience and my speech rolled out. When my voice stopped there was some applause. I did not care if they liked it or not; I was through. Immediately, even before I left the platform, I tried to shunt all memory of the event from me. A few of my classmates managed to shake my hand as I pushed toward the door, seeking the street. Somebody invited me to a party and I did not accept. I did not want to see any of them again. I walked home, saying to myself: The hell with it! With almost seventeen years of baffled living behind me, I faced the world in 1925.

DON'T FALL OFF THE MOUNTAIN
by Shirley MacLaine

Shirley MacLaine says that she was born into a cliché-loving, middle class family in Virginia. It would be hard, however, to describe her life in clichés.

Example. *Increasingly annoyed by a gossip columnist who over the years printed distasteful stories about her she claimed were false, she asked her attorney how she could "slug" someone without being sued for assault and battery. The reply: "If you hit with the flat of the hand instead of a balled up fist you don't commit assault and battery." She immediately called upon the offensive columnist in his office, and, in front of witnesses, hit him twice with the flat of her hand. President Kennedy telegraphed congratulations, and Governor Brown wired that he would referee any future fights for her.*

Example. *One of the ways she has always prepared for her parts has been by getting to know people typical of these roles. Her most unusual meeting came about when she signed to play "Irma La Douce", a Les Halles hooker with a heart of gold. With the son of French friends for interpreting and protection she wandered the side alleys adjacent to the old market place in Paris. There she met Danielle, who served as her role model.*

Example. *En route from Japan to America her plane stopped in Bombay where she planned to stay overnight. Instead, she remained three months. During that time she visited Bhutan, situated in the eastern Himalayas, land of hunger and disease, of intrigue and cruelty, of meditation and harmony.*

AN incident occurred when I was about sixteen that still blazes in my memory. I came home from a dancing-school rehearsal distraught because they had taken the role of Cinderella away from me for our Christmas production. Miss Day and Miss Gardiner said I had simply grown too tall, and that I looked clumsy.

I remember blurting it out in tears as I climbed the stairs to go to my room to be alone. Dad was coming down the stairs. He stopped, and with finger wagging told me that that should teach me to stop trying to do things I wasn't capable of. Wasn't this episode proof enough for me that, if I attempted to go beyond my range, I would only be crushed? Hadn't he told me many times during my life? When would I believe him? When would I understand that if I tried I would only be hurt?

It was like the time I sang "I Can't Say No" a few years before, at the entertainment assembly program. I had seen *Oklahoma* and fallen in love with the comedy character Ado Annie. I somehow felt I understood the level of her comedy. I put on a silly perky hat with a huge flower square on top and big clodhopper shoes, and when I did it at school everybody laughed—they really laughed. But Dad said I shouldn't be lulled into thinking that theirs was reliable laughter, that a high-school assembly wasn't the world, that I didn't know how to sing, and knew nothing about performing, and just because I had been tickled and moved by Celeste Holm didn't give me the right to take such a standard example of American musical comedy and desecrate it on the stage of Washington-Lee High School . . . . I never sang after that, not even "The Star-Spangled Banner" at assembly. I was too self-conscious. I thought he must be right. He said only people who had been taught things well and had been classically trained had the background to perform and be accepted. Naive, raw instinct was one thing, but it couldn't compare with traditional education. Only a fool would dare spread his arms wide, exposing his heart, and say—without training—"Here I am, World, I've got something to say." Only a deadhead would believe he could get away with that, because he'd get hurt—and hurt badly. And someone who might realize the pitfalls but say, "Up yours, World, I'm going to say it anyway," would have to be put away. Not only would he be insane—he'd be dangerous. He'd be dangerous because he was willing to be hurt.

I fell on the stairs, that December evening after rehearsal, with my father over me, berating me not only for trying to perform, but for thinking I could dance Cinderella, and for making a conspicuous ass out of myself as a result. And I cried hard—I cried so hard that I vomited. But the vomit on the stairs didn't stop him; he went right on driving home his point, that I would only be hurt if I dared to dare. I couldn't move. I looked over at Mother in the living room. Warren wasn't home. Mother sat quietly until finally she said, "All right, Ira, that's enough." But Ira knew that wasn't going to be the end of it. He could see, even though I had dissolved into a little pile of protoplasm, that I would never stop daring. And he seemed to understand that ironically he, in effect, was teaching me to dare because I saw that he was such a spectacular disappointment to himself for having never tried it. A strange clear look of understanding came into his eyes as he realized I didn't want to be like him. He stepped over the vomit and went to the kitchen to fix himself a drink. It was then that I determined to make the most of whatever equipment I had been born with, and part of that equipment was to dare. But mostly I didn't want to be a disappointment to myself.

TWO LEGS TO STAND ON
by John D. McKee

Handicapped (a word he shunned) by the spastic variety of cerebral palsy, John McKee fortunately did not have the double handicap of overly protective parents—more disabling than physical impairment. Once aware of their son's condition, his parents—concerned, devoted, strong in faith—moved persistently toward their goal: John's walking and enjoying normal life. To their "indomitable courage" John credits his full, active life. One cannot, however, ignore his own unconquerable courage, albeit inherited from and made easier by his parents.

McKee was born a few short years after World War I, a time when much less was known about cerebral palsy than now. The family doctor, well-intentioned but limited, told his parents that probably he would never walk and that he should not be exposed to surgery. His parents ignored this advice, and shortly before he was six he was operated upon. At six he walked for the first time. His spacicity had settled in his right leg and arm, and slightly in his left leg, but his left arm and speech were not impaired.

By the time he was nineteen he had had five operations. He claimed that these "have not given me normal legs, but they have given me a sure way of getting from one place to another." Further, as he points out, since the walking spastic has never known what it is to walk normally, "anything he learns to do from the time of his birth is bound to be an improvement over his original condition." Improvements for him over the years included walking three whole weeks without falling, reaching the top of banister-less stairs on hands and knees, teaching his right

105

*index finger—the only part of his right hand to escape
paralytic stiffness—to type.*

*When he was nearly twenty, a new world opened to him:
college. He was on his own.*

AS I stood on the steps of Pioneer Hall and looked north
up the broad brick expanse of Salina's Santa Fe Avenue, I
felt more alone than I had ever felt in my life before. The
year was 1939. I had gone down to Salina to enter Kansas
Wesleyan University. Dad had driven me there, had seen
me settled in a room just two blocks off campus, and had
brought me back to the administration building. Now the
beetlelike back of the maroon Ford was disappearing down
the avenue, and I was on my own.

It was the first time I had ever been really alone. By the
time Mother had left me in the hospital ward in Kansas
City, I had had time to make friends with the nurses and
the doctors and the other children in the ward. When I
went away to Scout camp, I went with the troop. There is
no time to be lonely in a Boy Scout camp. There is activity
all the time and there are new friends to be added to those
who come with you.

I was nearly twenty years old, then, when I was really on
my own for the first time in my life. I knew nobody, and
compared with Concordia, Salina was a big town. Only
three years before I had had what I hoped was my final
operation. Only a year before had I gone down into the
business district of Concordia alone. Always before, a
brother or a parent or a friend had been with me, to lean
on if need be, to help me cope with even small-town traffic. College life, regardless of what preparations I had
made for it, was bound to be a big, new, mysterious adventure nearly comparable with the adventure of my first
operation.

It was to be doubly an adventure for me because I had to learn to get around in a larger town. I had to learn to board and get off city buses in traffic. I had that familiar sick feeling in the pit of my stomach the first time I got on a bus at the college to ride downtown. What if I didn't get off at the right place? What if I lost my way once I got downtown? How would I find my way back to the campus? What would have been little decisions for anyone else, as far as getting away from the home base of the campus and my rooming house were concerned, were big decisions for me because I was making them for the first time in my life. I had to take my fear in my hands and go ahead and cross a downtown street, trusting that I would not fall in the middle of the street just as the traffic light changed. I had to find lampposts and fire hydrants to hold to as I pulled myself up tall curbings. When I came to an outside stairway without a wall or a banister to lean on, I had to study the situation as if it were an engineering problem to find a way to get up or down those stairs.

But all those problems were to present themselves, and be solved, later. Now, as Dad drove out of sight, I faced the compound of fear and loneliness that comes with tying off the cord to home.

I had come very near not going to college at all. What with the five times I had been in the hospital for operations and the cost of getting me through high school and the cost of my brothers' education, the burden of putting me through college might have been too much. Yet college had been in the back of all of our minds from the time I first signed up for college preparatory courses in my freshman year in high school. With the physical equipment I had—and didn't have—and with the high school training I had already received, further education seemed almost essential if I was to make anything out of my life.

Thanks to the Reverend Mr. Templin, minister of the First Methodist Church in Concordia, I had been offered a two-year scholarship at Kansas Wesleyan, but I couldn't accept it. Even with the scholarship, there wasn't enough money in the McKee till that year to get me through a year away from home. So I went back to high school and took some courses I had been unable to crowd into four years. And I waited. And sure enough, by the next fall Dad was running a grocery store in Glasco, Kansas, the family was on a better financial footing, and if I could get the remainder of that two-year scholarship, college would be possible.

So here I was, in the beginning of loneliness. But it was a loneliness that did not last long. Mr. and Mrs. L. A. Fox, with whom I roomed, were the kind of people a fellow naturally called "Dad" and "Mom." Dad Fox had an ironic sense of humor and a love of argument for the sake of argument. We listened to the fight broadcasts together and argued major league baseball and politics. The fact that we had such interests in common had much to do with making the home of the Foxes a second home to me.

I took my problems and my hopes to Mom Fox, and when a cold kept me in bed, she made sure I got my meals. I had a big square room. It was on the second floor of the house, but the stair railing was stout and I had a strong left arm to help pull me up the stairs and to steady me on the way down.

Once I was settled and had gotten over the shock of being born from the womb of home into a new world in which I had to stand immediately, like a calf, on my wobbly legs, I began to lay the boundaries of my world. There was Carlo Ramsey's University Cafe just down the block, and there was the barbershop where I went reluctantly every two weeks to be shorn. Every week I staggered, over-balanced, with my laundry and a letter home, to visit with the old lady who ran the combination branch post office and secondhand store. And when I had kicked the toes out of my shoes or the rubber heels were ground clear down to the leather on the inside, I walked the half a mile to the Wesleyan Shoe Shop to sit in my stocking feet and talk with the gap-toothed oldster whose careful hands and whirring power tools turned hopeless wrecks into new shoes, ready to be beaten and ground and kicked in by wayward feet for another two or three weeks.

The center of this world was, of course, the campus. There I found teachers whom I was to learn to revere in my four years at Wesleyan. I found others who acted as counterirritants and who served their purpose as if they had been good teachers. Once I was oriented in my world, I set about to do the things I could do. I crossed the tracks every afternoon I could during that first fall and went over to Glenn Martin Field to watch football practice, as I had gone to the high school field night after night while I was in high school. I volunteered a column to the Wesleyan *Advance* called "Sunflower Seeds," a column I was to write for four years. I answered the call for debaters.

Once away from home, I discovered that I could do many things which I had once thought impossible. At home when the weather was bad, be it from snow and ice or rain, Mother sometimes kept me home from school. At Wesleyan there was no one to keep me home, and I sallied forth in downpours and in snowdrifts. Except when the Smokey River flooded in 1941 the weather never kept me out of class. I was wet often, muddy often. I sometimes fell flat with an armful of books and scattered them over the ice and snow. Sometimes I sat soaking wet through all my classes before I could get home to change. I was foolhardy, inviting flu and pneumonia throughout the winter, but I was exhilarated by the freedom I had to try to keep a regular schedule and ignore the weather as the able-bodied did.

I found that I could go almost anywhere I wanted to go under my own power. Often when we had a better use for the nickel bus fare and the hitch-hiking was bad, a friend and I would walk the two miles to town. Impossible? Even a year before I went to Salina the idea would have been fantastic. Partly it was stubborness that made me do these things. I had to prove to myself that I could do them. For walking was to me what running would be for anyone else. In two blocks my body would be running with sweat, in six I could feel my pulse beating like a hammer in the back of my neck. But I knew that if I was not to have my life circumscribed by the little area I could cover comfortably, I would have to train myself to extend that area.

I don't suppose there were over four hundred students at Wesleyan at any one time during my four years there. The classes were small and so was the campus. Unless, wanting to be completely unhappy, you deliberately isolated yourself, you couldn't help making friends. Even if I had not since outgrown the introversion of my early teens, I could not have helped finding friends there. In such a small school, too, there is a personal relationship between student and instructor which makes for more individual development of any student's talent.

As in any small community, however, there were things and people at Wesleyan that were irksome. There is a certain necessary narrowness about a denominational school which will not admit of full exploration of ideas by an undergraduate, there were bigots on the faculty and among the students, but there were broad, big people there too, and the counterirritation was a valuable thing in sharing a philosophy.

In the end I had no more time to be lonely in college than I had had in Scout camp. I was never one to let my studies interefere with my education, and before I was through college I had edited the *Advance* for two years, worked in the college public relations office for three, organized the independents on campus, held office in the Forum Club and the Student Christian Movement, and been a member of a literary club, the Classical Club, and the campus Young Republicans. I had helped write the constitution for the men's dormitory and had been instrumental in getting a smoking room established there. I helped get social dancing established on the campus and made a little extra money by selecting the records and running the record player and the public address system at the dances. And I found time to write an honors paper in English and to preach a Mother's Day sermon in my roommate's country church.

I sometimes regretted that I hadn't had the chance to go to the state university and get a straight journalism degree, but I don't regret it any more. Besides the undeniably good feeling that comes from being a big frog in a little puddle, I received from my four years at Wesleyan a broad liberal education extending from literature through history, science, and international affairs to philosophy and religion. The knowledge of all these things plus the knowledge of people would serve me in good stead whether I stayed in journalism or attempted to go deeper and become a serious creative writer. I also tested further my own capacities, in a new environment and under varying circumstances. A person has to prove to himself what he can do. It's like dying; nobody can do it for you.

WOMEN OF CRISIS II
by Robert Coles and Jane Hallowell Coles

In Women of Crisis, *Robert Coles and Jane Hallowell Coles have presented "readings" of the lives of women with whom they have lived and worked. And from whom they have learned!*

Maria, a Pueblo, proved a powerful teacher. From her Robert and Jane Coles claimed that they not only learned about the Pueblo way "but about ourselves—what we thought of life, what we hoped for, very much feared, couldn't bear to consider, or regarded more intently, perhaps, than we realized."

Growing up, Maria felt truly herself only among the plants and animals and skies of the mesa, a flat-topped land form bounded by steep rock walls. At fourteen she refused to go back to school. On the mesa she met two young photographers—Anglos—who offered her a job as their assistant in Santa Fe. From them she learned to use a camera, and did so with intelligence and enthusiasm. She fell in love with one of the photographers but felt compelled to return home where for a time she endured the drudgery of endless household tasks. Eventually she fell in love with one of her own and married.

Maria proudly says, "I am a woman who is a Pueblo." She says her children ask "Are we really Pueblos?" She continues, "They see me selling Pueblo 'handicrafts,' and they ask me why. I tell them we are *Pueblo, and I sell what I make because I am proud I made it with my own hands, and because I want others to see and know what we as a people can do—try to make good, honest, lovely things;* and *because we need the money. Are we not also*

*Americans? . . . . I tell them all the time they are many
things; we all are; people on this earth, men or women or
children, Anglos or Spanish-speaking or Indians."*

WHEN Maria was twelve, she had awakened early one
morning; it was still dark, but the day was beginning to
make itself felt—the first, subtle light had made the
slightest inroad on the dark. She was relieved; she had
always, as far back as she could remember, feared the middle of the night. She lay there, listening: a coyote, birds
beginning to waken and talk, a breeze coming upon her.
She felt sick. She had a stomachache. She thought she was
being reclaimed: "I was sure that I wouldn't be Maria
when the sun came up. I was sure I'd be taken to the mesa,
and I'd meet a spirit, who would be the one inside me, and
we'd talk, and then I'd be there for a long time, and the
spirit would be with me, and no more reservation life for a
while! But I began to realize that it wasn't time; I was
going to be around for a long time. I was bleeding, as my
mother did! She had told me I would, and she was right.
She had told me to be glad, and there I was getting ready to
die and leave! Some of the older girls on the reservation
told us we'd soon be bleeding, and they told us we could
think of 'spirits' coming and going, or we could think of
ourselves as becoming women: the flesh, as the Anglo
priests in our Catholic Church put it! I wanted to go and
tell a priest what happened to me. I was sure he'd be
speechless. Priests don't like to be reminded of anything
connected to sex. When I told my mother of my idea, she
said I was a born troublemaker; and she reminded me
again that I'd come out feet first!"
    The mother had been comforting to Maria at the time of
her menarche. Before that they had not had much to do

with each other. The girl had argued with her father, sought the company of her uncle, listened intently to her grandfather—but, really, liked none of them at all. She had wondered whether she'd ever meet a man she'd like, then learn to trust. And she'd had no truck with the boys of her age. She was a loner, as her mother had noticed. Now, at twelve, the two of them could find themselves having a candid talk about the past—and not incidentally, getting a bit close for the first time: "My mother told me when I was born she knew I'd be the one to walk on my own, because my feet were already working before the rest of me came out. She told me that she kept looking at the feet when they held me up to her. The Anglo doctor told her she was 'wrong' to jump to her 'conclusion,' but she smiled to herself. I proved her right! I'd heard so much about my legs being born first that I would sometimes look at them as if they didn't belong to me, but were on their own! My mother told me, the time we had our first good talk, when my blood first showed, that we don't own ourselves, that the legs may be someone's spirit, that the blood coming may be someone's spirit calling to me.

"In school they teach you different ideas. I told my mother that the school nurse checked up on us, and always wanted to know about our 'periods.' A lot of the girls in my class had theirs before I got mine. I'll never forget the nurse telling me that Indians are dark, and we get our 'periods' before they do, the Anglos. I looked at her, and there she was: light hair and her eyes blue. I wanted to ask her how old she was when she got hers, but I said nothing. She told the teacher that I was a 'strange one,' because I didn't talk, I did talk, but not to her!

"I talked a long time with my mother that day. I told her what the nurse had said. For the first time in my life, the only time in my life, one of my parents talked honestly about the Anglos and the Pueblos, and what it's like to be a Pueblo among the Anglos, and what it's like to be a Pueblo woman. I sat there, hearing about the history of our people—how we fought the Spanish, but were not warriors, and only wanted peace, so that we could grow food and live quietly and take care of the land we lived on and the land nearby. My mother said some of the Pueblo men worry about the past: should they have fought harder? How hard should you fight, when another people show up, and they can wipe you out with their guns, because they live to fight and win and strip you clean, and you live to grow food and teach your children to say yes to the sun, yes to the sky, yes to the land, yes to all the world? My mother said that for a long time the Pueblos have gone back and forth between the Anglo cities and their own land, and it's been hard, but with each child there's a chance to be a *Pueblo*, not a reservation Indian who belongs to the Anglos—their children who start bleeding early, because they are dark!''

What does it mean to be a Pueblo? A Pueblo woman? Maria wanted to know, badly wanted to know. The mother was a bit put off by the ardent nature of the child's curiosity—as the child would never forget: "That was a hot afternoon: May, early summer. My mother told me I was making it hotter, with all my questions! I kept asking her about herself and her sister. She had one sister who left the reservation, and married an Anglo, and came back every year or so for a visit. My mother didn't want to talk about her sister. She didn't want to go on talking about the Anglos, either. She said that the best thing we can do is keep the Anglos out of our home—not mention them. When I asked her why her sister would ever want to marry an Anglo, she said she didn't know. But I asked again, and finally she told me what she thought—that her sister always liked to be different, and was always hiding, or taking long walks by herself, and later she met an Anglo who was fixing the road that goes from our reservation to the state highway, and they started going out, and that was how it happened.

"I wanted to know more! I guess I already knew more! I guess I wanted to hear my mother say what I knew—but she wouldn't. She never talked with me about sex. She was from another generation. Actually, I'm the only one in my family, of *my* generation, who will talk about sex. My sisters won't use the word! They say I've become an Anglo! They say I know too much about the Anglo world! But they have television sets, and they have eyes, and they have ears! Back then, when I was twelve, we had no television set, and my mother was really upset when I asked if her sister had a baby before she married the Anglo. She asked me where I got the idea. I told her I was her daughter, and I knew that babies don't just fall from the sky! Hadn't she told me all these years how *I* was born? That was when she took me and hugged me, and said I should be careful, because 'once a man gets to you, that's the start of a new life, and you're never the same!' "

"My mother is a believing Catholic. I have never agreed with her on the subject of sex. I loved that talk with her—hearing from her own lips what she believed. But I knew that would be not only the first but the last real talk we'd have. She kept touching my arm and telling me not to 'worry' because the blood would only come for a day or two, and about as often as a full moon. I wasn't 'worried'; I was interested in what my life would be like, later on. My mother had the answer for me: a Pueblo man like my father would be my life! But my father was always telling me to behave myself, and stop running away to the mesa! I was not his favorite; the boys were! I almost asked my mother why she let my father be so unfair with his attention, but I couldn't get the words out of my mouth. I saw the answer in her eyes: don't ask me, because once I start asking myself a landslide will begin, and I won't be fast enough to get out of the way! As I sat there, glad to have a chance at least to be alone with my mother, I remembered the time I saw the rocks falling down off the mountains nearby, and the poor goats trying to escape. The birds were safe! I've wanted all my life to be a bird, the next time around—if there will be another chance!''

DAVID
The Old Testament

David, the greatest of Israel's kings and successor to Saul,
ruled the ancient Hebrews for thirty-three years. During
his reign the Jews progressed from a somewhat loose con-
federation of tribes to a more settled national state. David
moved his capital from Hebron to Jerusalem.

As a youth he became known for the sweetness of his
music, and many of the Psalms are ascribed to him. He
figures in some of the most moving Biblical narratives—his
friendship with Jonathan, his lamentation for his dead
son, Absalom, as well as the following account.

NOW the Philistines gathered together their armies to battle, and were gathered together at Shochoh, which
belongeth to Judah, and pitched between Shochoh and
Azekah, in Ephesdammin.

And Saul and the men of Israel were gathered together,
and pitched by the valley of Elah, and set the battle in
array against the Philistines.

And the Philistines stood on a mountain on the one side,
and Israel stood on a mountain on the other side: and there
was a valley between them.

And there went out a champion out of the camp of the
Philistines, named Goliath, of Gath, whose height was six
cubits and a span.

And he had a helmet of brass upon his head, and he was
armed with a coat of mail; and the weight of the coat was
five thousand shekels of brass.

And he had greaves of brass upon his legs, and a target
of brass between his shoulders.

And the staff of his spear was like a weaver's beam, and

his spear's head weighed six hundred shekels of iron: and one bearing a shield went before him.

And he stood and cried unto the armies of Israel, and said unto them, Why are ye come out to set your battle in array? am not I a Philistine, and ye servants to Saul? choose you a man for you, and let him come down to me.

If he be able to fight with me, and to kill me, then will we be your servants: but if I prevail against him, and kill him, then shall ye be our servants, and serve us.

And the Philistine said, I defy the armies of Israel this day: give me a man, that we may fight together.

When Saul and all Israel heard those words of the Philistine, they were dismayed, and greatly afraid.

Now David was the son of that Ephrathite of Bethlehemjudah, whose name was Jesse; and he had eight sons: and the man went among men for an old man in the days of Saul.

And the three eldest sons of Jesse went and followed Saul to the battle: and the names of his three sons that went to the battle were Eliab the first-born; the next unto him, Abinadab; and the third, Shammah.

And David was the youngest: and the three eldest followed Saul.

But David went and returned from Saul to feed his father's sheep at Bethlehem.

And the Philistine drew near morning and evening, and presented himself forty days.

And Jesse said unto David his son, Take now for thy brethren an ephah of this parched corn, and these ten loaves, and run to the camp to thy brethren.

And carry these ten cheeses unto the captain of their thousand, and look how thy brethren fare, and take their pledge.

Now Saul, and they, and all of the men of Israel, were in

the valley of Elah, fighting with the Philistines.

And David rose up early in the morning, and left the sheep with a keeper, and went, as Jesse had commanded him; and he came to the trench, as the host was going forth to the fight, and shouted for the battle.

For Israel and the Philistines had put the battle in array, army against army.

And David left his carriage in the hand of the keeper of the carriage, and ran into the army, and came and saluted his brethren.

And as he talked with them, behold, there came up the champion (the Philistine of Gath, Goliath by name) out of the armies of the Philistines, and spake according to the same words: and David heard them.

And all the men of Israel, when they saw the man, fled from him, and were sore afraid.

And the men of Israel said, Have ye seen this man that is come up? surely to defy Israel is he come up; and it shall be, that the man who killeth him, the king will enrich him with great riches, and will give him his daughter, and make his father's house free in Israel.

And David spake to the men that stood by him, saying, What shall be done to the man that killeth this Philistine, and taketh away the reproach from Israel? for who is this uncircumcised Philistine, that he should defy the armies of the living God?

And the people answered him after this manner, saying, So shall it be done to the man that killeth him.

And Eliab, his eldest brother, heard when he spake unto the man; and Eliab's anger was kindled against David, and he said, Why camest thou down hither? and with whom hast thou left those few sheep in the wilderness? I know thy pride, and the naughtiness of thine heart; for thou are come down that thou mightest see the battle.

And David said, What have I now done? Is there not a cause?

And he turned from him toward another, and spake after the same manner: and the people answered him again after the former manner.

And when the words were heard which David spake, they rehearsed them before Saul: and he sent for him.

And David said to Saul, Let no man's heart fail because of him: thy servant will go and fight with this Philistine.

And Saul said to David, Thou art not able to go against this Philistine to fight with him; for thou art but a youth, and he a man of war from his youth.

And David said unto Saul, Thy servant kept his father's sheep, and there came a lion, and a bear, and took a lamb out of the flock;

And I went out after him, and smote him, and delivered it out of his mouth: and when he arose against me, I caught him by his beard, and smote him, and slew him.

Thy servant slew both the lion and the bear; and this uncircumcised Philistine shall be as one of them, seeing he hath defied the armies of the living God.

David said moreover, The LORD that delivered me out of the paw of the lion, and out of the paw of the bear, he will deliver me out of the hand of this Philistine. And Saul said unto David, Go, and the LORD be with thee.

And Saul armed David with his armour, and he put a helmet of brass upon his head; also he armed him with a coat of mail.

And David girded his sword upon his armour, and he assayed to go; for he had not proved it. And David said unto Saul, I cannot go with these; for I have not proved them. And David put them off him.

And he took his staff in his hand, and chose him five smooth stones out of the brook, and put them in a shepherd's bag which he had, even in a scrip; and his sling was in his hand; and he drew near to the Philistine.

And the Philistine came on, and drew near unto David; and the man that bare the shield went before him.

And when the Philistine looked about, and saw David, he disdained him; for he was but a youth, and ruddy, and of a fair countenance.

And the Philistine said unto David, Am I a dog, that thou comest to me with staves? And the Philistine cursed David by his gods.

And the Philistine said to David, Come to me, and I will give thy flesh unto the fowls of the air, and to the beasts of the field.

Then said David to the Philistine, Thou comest to me with a sword, and with a spear, and with a shield: but I come to thee in the name of the LORD of hosts, the God of the armies of Israel, whom thou hast defied.

This day will the LORD deliver thee into mine hand; and I will smite thee, and take thine head from thee; and I will give the carcases of the host of the Philistines this day unto the fowls of the air, and to the wild beasts of the earth; that all the earth may know that there is a God in Israel.

And all this assembly shall know that the LORD saveth not with sword and spear; for the battle is the LORD'S, and he will give you into our hands.

And it came to pass, when the Philistine arose, and came and drew nigh to meet David, that David hasted, and ran toward the army to meet the Philistine.

And David put his hand in his bag, and took thence a stone, and slang it, and smote the Philistine in his forehead, that the stone sunk into his forehead; and he fell upon his face to the earth.

So David prevailed over the Philistine with a sling and

with a stone, and smote the Philistine, and slew him; but there was no sword in the hand of David.

Therefore David ran, and stood upon the Philistine, and took his sword, and drew it out of the sheath thereof, and slew him, and cut off his head therewith. And when the Philistines saw their champion was dead, they fled.

And the men of Israel and of Judah arose, and shouted, and pursued the Philistines, until thou come to the valley, and to the gates of Ekron; and the wounded of the Philistines fell down by the way to Shaaraim, even unto Gath, and unto Ekron.

And the children of Israel returned from chasing after the Philistines, and they spoiled their tents.

And David took the head of the Philistine, and brought it to Jerusalem: but he put his armour in his tent.

And when Saul saw David go forth against the Philistine, he said unto Abner, the captain of the host, Abner, whose son is this youth? And Abner said, As thy soul liveth, O king, I cannot tell.

And the king said, Inquire thou whose son the stripling is.

And as David returned from the slaughter of the Philistine, Abner took him, and brought him before Saul with the head of the Philistine in his hand.

And Saul said to him, Whose son art thou, thou young man? And David answered, I am the son of thy servant Jesse the Bethlehemite.

SIXTEEN
by Maureen Daly

Maureen Daly was sixteen when she wrote "Sixteen." And that was more than forty years ago. Yet were it not for certain dated indications of an era past—Walter Winchell, Wayne King, Joseph Stalin, everyone's wearing saddle shoes and sipping lemon cokes—you might think that the story had just been written today. Or that it might be written tomorrow. Conversational exchanges are the same, as are the emotions, the hopes, the disappointment.

Although born in Ireland, the author grew up in a small Wisconsin town. There were four girls in the family, little money, and much ambition. Growing up, coming of age—these were to be savored. Among the things important were (in whatever order you wish) books, boys, family. The central figure was Mrs. Daly.

Each of the four girls pursued successful careers in some way involving writing. Maureen followed her prize-winning "Sixteen" with an acclaimed novel, Seventeenth Summer, *published before she finished college. A romantic, she was also a pragmatist. She and I were college classmates at Rosary College in suburban Chicago. I still have a vivid picture of her sitting at a table in the college grill correcting her letters from a boy back home very much in love with her.*

In "Sixteen" both the romantic and the pragmatist show through.

NOW don't get me wrong. I mean, I want you to understand from the beginning that I'm not really so dumb. I know what a girl should do and what she shouldn't. I get around. I read. I listen to the radio. And I have two older sisters. So you see, I know what the score is. I know it's smart to wear tweedish skirts and shaggy sweaters with the sleeves pushed up and pearls and ankle socks and saddle shoes that look as if they've seen the world. And I know that your hair should be long, almost to your shoulders, and sleek as a wet seal, just a little fluffed on the ends and you should wear a campus hat or a dink or else a peasant hankie if you've that sort of face. Properly, a peasant hankie should make you think of edelweiss, mist and sunny mountains, yodeling and Swiss cheese. You know, that kind of peasant. Now, me, I never wear a hankie. It makes my face seem wide and Slavic and I look like a picture always in one of those magazine articles that run—"And Stalin says the future of Russia lies in its women. In its women who have tilled its soil, raised its children—" Well, anyway. I'm not exactly too small town either. I read Winchell's column. You get to know what New York boy is that way about some pineapple princess on the West Coast and what Paradise pretty is currently the prettiest and why someone, eventually, will play Scarlett O'Hara. It gives you that cosmopolitan feeling. And I know that anyone who orders a strawberry sundae in a drugstore instead of a lemon coke would probably be dumb enough to wear colored ankle socks with high-heeled pumps or use Evening in Paris with a tweed suit. But I'm sort of drifting. This isn't what I wanted to tell you. I just wanted to give you the general idea of how I'm not so dumb. It's important that you understand that.

You see, it was funny how I met him. It was a winter night like any other winter night. And I didn't have my Latin done either. But the way the moon tinseled the twigs and silver-plated the snow drifts, I just couldn't stay inside. The skating rink isn't far from our house—you can make it in five minutes if the sidewalks aren't slippery, so I went skating. I remember it took me a long time to get ready that night because I had to darn my skating socks first. I don't know why they always wear out so fast—just in the toes too. Maybe it's because I have metal protectors on the toes of my skates. That probably *is* why. And then I brushed my hair—hard, so hard it clung to my hand and stood up around my head in a hazy halo.

My skates were hanging by the back door all nice and shiny for I'd just gotten them for Christmas and they smelled so queer—just like fresh smoked ham. My dog walked with me as far as the corner. She's a red Chow, very polite and well-mannered, and she kept pretending it was me she liked when all the time I knew it was the ham smell. She panted along beside me and her hot breath made a frosty little balloon balancing on the end of her nose. My skates thumped me good-naturedly on my back as I walked and the night was breathlessly quiet and the stars winked down like a million flirting eyes. It was all so lovely.

It was all so lovely I ran most of the way and it was lucky the sidewalks had ashes on them or I'd have slipped surely. The ashes crunched like cracker-jack and I could feel their cindery shape through the thinness of my shoes. I always wear old shoes when I go skating.

I had to cut across someone's back garden to get to the rink and last summer's grass stuck through the thin ice, brown and discouraged. Not many people came through this way and the crusted snow broke through the little hollows between corn stubbles frozen hard in the ground. I was out of breath when I got to the shanty—out of breath with running and with the loveliness of the night. Shanties are always such friendly places. The floor all hacked to wet splinters from the skate runners and the wooden wall frescoed with symbols of dead romance. There was a smell of singed wool as someone got too near the glowing isinglass grin of the iron stove. Girls burst through the door laughing with snow on their hair and tripped over shoes scattered on the floor. A pimply-faced boy grabbed the hat from the frizzled head of an eighth-grade blonde and stuffed it into an empty galosh to prove his love and then hastily bent to examine his skate strap with innocent unconcern.

It didn't take me long to get my own skates on and I stuck my shoes under the bench—far back where they wouldn't get knocked around and would be easy to find when I wanted to go home. I walked out on my toes and the shiny runners of my new skates dug deep into the sodden floor.

It was snowing a little outside—quick, eager little Lux-like flakes that melted as soon as they touched your hand. I don't know where the snow came from for there were stars out. Or maybe the stars were in my eyes and I just kept seeing them every time I looked up into the darkness. I waited a moment. You know, to start to skate at a crowded rink is like jumping on a moving merry-go-round. The skaters go skimming round in a colored blur like gaudy painted horses and the shrill musical jabber re-echoes in the night from a hundred human calliopes. Once in, I went all right. At least after I found out exactly where that rough ice was. It was "round, round, jump the rut, round, round, round, jump the rut, round, round—"

And then he came. All of a sudden his arm was around my waist so warm and tight and he said very casually, "Mind if I skate with you?" and then he took my other hand. That's all there was to it. Just that and then we were skating. It wasn't that I'd never skated with a boy before. Don't be silly. I told you before I get around. But this was different. He was a smoothie! He was a big shot up at school and he went to all the big dances and he was the best dancer in town except Harold Wright who didn't count because he'd been to college in New York for two years! Don't you see? This was different.

At first I can't remember what we talked about, I can't even remember if we talked at all. We just skated and skated and laughed every time we came to that rough spot and pretty soon we were laughing all the time at nothing at all. It was all so lovely.

Then we sat on the big snow bank at the edge of the rink and just watched. It was cold at first even with my skating pants on, sitting on that hard heap of snow but pretty soon I got warm all over. He threw a handful of snow at me and it fell in a little white shower on my hair and he leaned over to brush it off. I held my breath. The night stood still.

The moon hung just over the warming shanty like a big quarter slice of muskmelon and the smoke from the pipe chimney floated up in a sooty fog. One by one the houses around the rink twinked out their lights and somebody's hound wailed a mournful apology to a star as he curled up for the night. It was all so lovely.

Then he sat up straight and said, "We'd better start home." Not "Shall I take you home?" or "Do you live far?" but "We'd better start home." See, that's how I know he wanted to take me home. Not because he *had* to but because he *wanted* to. He went to the shanty to get my shoes. "Black ones," I told him. "Same size as Garbo's." And he laughed again. He was still smiling when he came back and took off my skates and tied the wet skate strings in a soggy knot and put them over his shoulder. Then he held out his hand and I slid off the snow bank and brushed off the seat of my pants and we were ready.

It was snowing harder now. Big, quiet flakes that clung to twiggy bushes and snuggled in little drifts against the tree trunks. The night was an etching in black and white. It was all so lovely I was sorry I lived only a few blocks away. He talked softly as we walked as if every little word were a secret. "Did I like Wayne King, and did I plan to go to college next year and had I a cousin who lived in Appleton and knew his brother?" A very respectable Emily Post sort of conversation and then finally—"how nice I looked with snow in my hair and had I ever seen the moon so—close?" For the moon was following us as we walked and ducking playfully behind a chimney every time I turned to look at it. And then we were home.

The porch light was on. My mother always puts the porch light on when I go away at night. And we stood there a moment by the front steps and the snow turned pinkish in the glow of the colored light and a few feathery flakes settled on his hair. Then he took my skates and put them over my shoulder and said, "Good night now. I'll call you." "I'll call you," he said.

I went inside then and in a moment he was gone. I watched him from my window as he went down the street. He was whistling softly and I waited until the sound faded away so I couldn't tell if it was he or my heart whistling out there in the night. And then he was gone, completely gone.

I shivered. Somehow the darkness seemed changed. The stars were little hard chips of light far up in the sky and the moon stared down with a sullen yellow glare. The air was tense with sudden cold, and a gust of wind swirled his footprints into white oblivion. Everything was quiet.

But he'd said, "I'll call you." That's what he said, "I'll call you." I couldn't sleep all night.

And that was last Thursday. Tonight is Tuesday. Tonight is Tuesday and my homework's done, and I darned some stockings that didn't really need it, and I worked a crossword puzzle, and I listened to the radio and now I'm just sitting. I'm just sitting because I can't think of anything else to do. I can't think of anything, anything but snowflakes and ice skates and yellow moons and Thursday night. The telephone is sitting on the corner table with its old black face turned to the wall so I can't see its leer. I don't even jump when it rings any more. My heart still prays but my mind just laughs. Outside the night is still, so still I think I'll go crazy and the white snow's all dirtied and smoked into grayness and the wind is blowing the arc light so it throws weird, waving shadows from the trees onto the lawn—like thin, starved arms begging for I don't know what. And so I'm just sitting here and I'm not feeling anything. I'm not even sad because all of a sudden I know. All of a sudden I know. I can sit here now forever and laugh and laugh and laugh while the tears run salty in the corners of my mouth. For all of a sudden I know, I know what the stars knew all the time—he'll never, never call—never.

PICTURES IN THE HALLWAY
by Sean O'Casey

Sean O'Casey's multi-volumed autobiography is considered one of the classics of the genre. He opens it this way: "In Dublin, sometime in the early 1880's, on the last day of the month of March, a mother in child-pain clenched her teeth, dug her knees home into the bed, sweated and panted and grunted, became a tense living mass of agony and effort, groaned and pressed and groaned and pressed and pressed a little boy out of her womb into a world where white and black horses and brown and white horses trotted tap-tap-tap tap-tap-tappety-tap over cobblestones, conceitedly, in front of landau, brougham, or vis-a-vis; lumberingly in front of tramcar; pantingly and patiently in front of laden lorry, dray or float; and gaily in front of the merry and irresponsible jaunting-car."

The mother and father named the new child John although the mother had misgivings. She had two sons dead, each of whom had been named John. She did not want to seem to be challenging God, but her husband said that this last boy's name was to be John, too. The John often turned into Johnny as he grew up in the slums of Dublin. And he ended up Sean O'Casey, one of Ireland's greatest dramatists, his plays including Juno and the Paycock, *and* The Plough and the Stars.

JOHNNY was getting on in years now, growing old with the world and all who were in it. Lean and lanky he grew, with masses of hair growing low down in front, that his mother laboured to brush back from his forehead, saying he'd look as if he knew nothing if he hadn't a high brow. A few days before his fourteenth birthday, he could manage to read, skipping the biggest words, the stories in *The Boys of London and New York*, and the various coloured-cover penny adventure books, and *Ally Sloper*, a weekly comic, whenever he had the penny to spare for one of them. So, if you ask me, he knew nearly as much as there was to be known, and fit he was to take his place in the world, paddle his own canoe, and fill a job with the best boy going, as soon as he could get one. Every day Archie carefully scanned the "Situations Vacant" columns of the *Daily Express*, on the lookout for a suitable chance for Johnny.

Early on one fair morning in April, Johnny was wakened by having his shoulder shaken by his mother.

—Get up, she said, get up, like a good boy, for Archie has just come across the very thing for you.

Johnny slowly opened his sleep-dim eyes and murmured, Let him speak, for I can hear as well lyin' down as I can sittin' up.

—Get up, get up, man, said Archie impatiently; and when you've washed your face you'll be betther able to take in what I've got to say to you.

Johnny got up, dressed, and washed his face, wondering how he could be able to understand better when all this had been done. Then he sat down by the fire to listen to what the one and only Archie had to say.

Archie opened out the *Daily Express* and looked earnestly into it. Then, in a stately and dignified voice, he read, A smart, respectable, and honest boy wanted. One just finished school preferred. Apply by letter to Hymdim, Leadem & Co., Henry Street, Dublin. There y'are, he added, the chance of a lifetime.

—Maybe a godsend, said his mother.

—A fine big Firm, said Archie, one o' th' biggest in th'

whole city, an' protestant to the backbone.

—Johnny'll never know what he'll rise to, in a Firm like that, murmured the mother.

—Let him run down, now, to Ella, an' get her to write out a letther for him, applyin' for the job; an' another of her own as a schoolmisthress, sayin' Johnny was a good boy, an' most attentive to his studies, instructed Archie. Let her just sign it E. Benson, so as to show no sign that it was written by a woman.

—An' I'll ask Mrs. Middleton for the loan of her boy's new topcoat, said Mrs. Casside, for Johnny to have a betther chance of lookin' the boy the job was meant for; an', if he gets the job, we can get one for himself at a bob a week from oul' Greenberg. Hurry off, now, she said to Johnny, to your sisther, an' get her to write the two letthers; on your way there, buyin' a pennorth o' notepaper an' envelopes, a penny bottle of ink, an' a ha'penny pen, in case Ella 'ud be empty-handed. Then hurry back; I'll have th' coat waitin' for you, an' you can go at once and see if they'll give you th' job.

Johnny girded up his loins and set off at a quick walk to his sister's place in Summerhill, popping into a shop on the way and buying all he needed; quickening the walk to a quicker trot, then to the quickest gallop; sliding down, after a while, to a trot, then to a quick walk for a rest; then breaking into a gallop again, going on like Paul Revere to tell the town the enemy was on the way, till he came panting to his sister, showed her the news his mother had cut from the paper, and telling her what she had to do.

In a hurry, she washed her hands for fear of soiling the letter, and saying that when it was written he'd have to copy what she had written, for they'd know her neat hand was hardly the hand of a schoolboy. So when she had written, Johnny, with his face screwed up, and with much labour and care, wrote in a large-lettered hand, the following:

Dear Sirs,
    I have observed by an advertisement appearing in the *Daily Express* of this morning's issue, that your Firm is in need of an honest, smart, and respectable boy, and that you prefer to employ one who has just finished school. I venture to say that I have all the qualities required, and, as I have just left school, I beg to offer myself as a candidate for the position.
Very respectfully yours,
JOHN CASSIDE
Messrs. Hymdim & Leadem.

Ella then wrote on another sheet of notepaper:

St. Mary's National School,
Lr. Dominick Street.
    The Bearer, John Casside, has been a pupil in the above school, during which period I have always found him a truthful, honest, and obedient boy, and, at all times, most attentive to his studies. I feel sure he will give perfect satisfaction to any employer good enough to use his services.
E. Benson,
School Teacher

Johnny hurried home with the letters; dressed himself in all his faded finery, putting the almost new blue Melton coat, loaned to his mother by Mrs. Middleton, over the lot, and hastened off to join those who were busy battling with the world.

When he came to Sackville Street, he felt hot and a little out of breath. He felt the sweat oozing out between his thighs, making his trousers feel a little damp. He had gone too quickly, he thought. His stomach felt as full as if he had just eaten a great meal, but he had had only a cup of tea and a cut of dry bread. Tight it felt as a tightly laced drum. If he could only pop into the job, without having to see anyone about it. Still, he was here, and in he'd have to go, and finish what he had begun. But better wait till he had cooled down a little; never do to show you were in a sweat to get it. Go in, cool and collected, and appear as if you didn't care whether you got it or not: and had just dropped in because you had nothing else to do, and the day was long. He'd sit here for a few seconds, till his heart got down to a quieter beat, and then go on: forward—the Buffs! He sat down on one of the pedestals of one of the General Post Office's great pillars, listening to the tram timekeeper, a brown-bearded man, wearing a half tall hat, calling out for the trams to make a start: Sandymount, and away would go that tram; Palmerston Park, and away would go that tram too, with a tinkle from the bell the conductor pulled. All aboard for Palmerston Park, where the gentry lived. Most of them were moving to where the gentry lived, passing through the poorer quarters, out to where there were trees, air, and sunshine, where the gentry lived.

For the tenth time, Johnny took the letters from his pocket and read them, before he finally sealed them up for ever. Not so bad, he said, as he licked the flaps and closed them down, for if they want a genuinely honest, truthful, and willing boy, they needn't look over my shoulder for one.

He watched for a few more moments the soldiers streaming past him: Hussars, in their gorgeous crimson trousers; Army Service Corps, with their sober blue-and-white uniforms; Lancers, white-breasted, red-breasted, or yellow-breasted; Guards, in their tight little trousers, tight little white pea-jackets, tight little caps; Highlanders, with their kilts swinging—all on the hunt for girls; always strolling on the same side of the street, the west side, never on the other, where all the respectable people walked who didn't like to make contact with a common soldier; from the corner of Great Britain Street, principally, to the Royal Bank of Ireland, back and forward, stopping when they made a catch, restlessly moving backwards and forwards, on the hunt for girls.

> While up the street, each girl they meet,
> Will look so shy, then cry, my eye!
> Och! Isn't he a darling,
> Me bould sodger boy!

He felt quite cool, now, so he licked three of his fingers, and smoothed his hair back from his forehead as far as it would go. He dusted the seat of his trousers, felt that his Eton collar sat still and safe, pulled the lapels of his blue Melton coat forward, and sallied up Henry Street, threading his way through the crowds of people coming out and going into shops. Right into the big store he dived, asking where he could deliver a letter that answered an advertisement wanting a truthful, honest, and willing boy. The far end of the great shop was pointed out to him, and he was told that when he passed through a door there, he would find a Mr. Anthony who would deal with the matter contained in the letter applying for the post. So Johnny went on a long journey by steep mountains of chandlery, terraces of lamps of every sort, table lamps, tiny lamps, bracket, hanging, hall, and reading lamps; small wick, wide wick, single wick, and double wick lamps; forest of brushes, hair, fibre, and twig; valleys of curtains, cloth, beads, and bamboo; huge rockeries of ironmongery; while overhead was a great gallery, circling the whole of the ground floor, filled with all kinds of delft and chinaware, beetling over all as if eager to look at all the other wonders piled in the valley below. Through all these he wended his way to a glass-panelled door leading to the packing and despatch departments. Pushing this open, he came into a long dark store, holding all the future supplies for the shop inside, and divided into heavy benches on which goods were piled, to be parcelled and packed and sent to various parts of the city and suburbs. On one side of this store, near the glass-panelled door, was a boxed-in office, full of windows, so that everything everywhere could be seen by a tiny lift of the head of anyone who might happen to be in it. In this office was a tall lean man, with a head like a fairly thin egg, whose hair began to sprout in the middle of his head, giving him the look of a waning scholar, who glanced up and looked at Johnny with a keen look in a pair of watery eyes that were thinly blue in colour.

Johnny, with his cap held respectfully under his arm, handed the two letters to this man, who was Anthony Dovergull, one of two brothers, owners of this big Firm of Messrs. Hymdim, Leadem & Company; the other brother (Johnny found out afterwards) was as jet-black as this one was fair, with a heavy moustache losing itself in a heavy coal-black beard (his brother was clean-shaven), with brilliant black eyes that never knew how to soften. He was as tall as his fair brother, but had thick legs, massive shoulders, like a bull's, that gathered together and bent, when he was angry, like a bull about to charge; and his only smile, seen when the House was doing good business, was like a wintry sunbeam finding a home in an icicle. The dark fellow watched over the front of the Firm, standing on a bridge stretching from one side of the chinaware gallery to the other, stood all the day like a skipper on the bridge of a ship.

Mr. Anthony Dovergull took the letters from Johnny, read them silently, and looked Johnny all over. Johnny was glad that he had Middleton's Melton overcoat on him. Then Mr. Anthony read the letters again, thought for a moment or two; then looked at Johnny again.

—You are a protestant, young man, are you not? he asked.

—Oh yes, of course, sir, answered Johnny, feeling that he had a close kinship with the mighty man in the boxed-in office.

—Well, we'll try you, said Mr. Anthony. You can start tomorrow morning. Hours, eight till six; wages, three shillings, and sixpence a week; rising, of course, annually, if your services are found to be satisfactory. And he dismissed Johnny by turning to resume the work he had been doing when Johnny handed him the letters.

So here he was standing in the street again, a child of fortune, a member of Hymdim, Leadem & Company, and an inheritor of three shillings and sixpence a week. He had made a flying start. He would begin life at eight o'clock the following morning. In the morning his life would break into bud. Aaron's rod all over again; it would bud and blossom. He was a child no longer. He had put childish things far from him. He was a worker. Henceforth he would earn his bread in the sweat of his face. The earth was his, and the fulness thereof. Glory be to God. Out of the darkness had come a saving light.

And Johnny felt that it was good; and the morning and the evening were the fair'st day.

CHANGE LOBSTERS—AND DANCE
by Lilli Palmer

Lilli Palmer's father, a Berlin doctor, named her after Goethe's young love, Lili Schonemann, but the registrar added an extra "l" to the birth record. Her autobiography gets its title from "The Lobster-Quadrille" in Alice's Adventures in Wonderland. *The Mock Turtle says to Alice, "You may not have lived much under the sea and perhaps you were never even introduced to a lobster so you can have no idea what a delightful thing a Lobster-Quadrille is."*

Lilli claimed that she and her two sisters owed their "happy childhood to the fact that my parents made no secret of loving each other more than they loved us. They were devoted to us, worried over us, were sometimes proud of us, but on the whole they were interested in each other first and us second. As a result there was a relaxed, balanced climate of independence, where nobody felt 'loved' obsessively or possessively."

Although her father wanted her to be a doctor, there was never any doubt in Lilli's mind that she would become an actress. Each phase of her life had helped to develop her as such. A most important influence was Elsa Schreiber, her acting coach in London. From her she learned "how to work on a role, how never to lose sight of the story line or the character." She learned too that talent meant nothing if you did not also have what Elsa called "staying power."

As an international actress of the stage and screen Lilli Palmer has acted with, among others, Rex Harrison (to whom she was once married), Gary Cooper, Noel Coward,

Clark Gable, Fred Astaire and William Holden. In addition to her acting, she has established herself as an artist and writer.

EVEN before I presented myself, radiant and excited, at the office of the State Theater of Darmstadt (one of the best repertory companies in Germany) on August 1, 1932, things had begun to simmer and bubble in the political life of the nation. Suddenly people were actually reading those ridiculous newspapers published by the Nazi party, instead of just making fun of them. My father, with his love of Germany, refused to believe that his country would ever allow itself to be represented by "that kind of man." And when he was finally forced to recognize that Germany would indeed allow it, he sought refuge in the hope that, once in the saddle, "that man" would drop his mad ideas and "behave decently," as befitted the leader of a civilized country. It never occured to my father to emigrate. As chief of surgery at Berlin's biggest Jewish hospital, he was irreplaceable anyway.

In those early days only a few farsighted people thought of moving to another country. Those few closed their bank accounts, packed their belongings, and left Germany as if an alarm bell had sounded. The majority stayed where they were and waited.

My salary was tiny, a hundred and twenty-five marks a month. After all, I was a beginner, just turned eighteen. My father added another hundred so that I could live, though only just. "I don't want to stand in your way," he had said when I triumphantly showed him my Darmstadt contract, "but I still don't think you'll last long on the stage."

"Oh, yes, I will, Vati," I exclaimed. "All of my life!"

I was immediately put to work in all kinds of productions. Unfortunately I could dance and sing a little, and that was my undoing. I was cast in musical comedies, although neither my dancing nor my singing was even halfway adequate. *White Horse Inn*, for instance, was going into its third season in the repertory of every German theater, and twice a week I "sang" in that. Since my numbers placed me opposite the tenor who sang Tristan on other nights, nobody was surprised that my voice never quite came across.

I also appeared as Stasi in Kalman's *Gypsy Princess*, a role that includes several world-famous songs. I managed to scrape through because the conductor was used to my "voice" and held the orchestra down to a mere whisper whenever I opened my mouth. Suddenly an SOS came from nearby Frankfurt. They, too, were doing *The Gypsy Princess* at their opera house, and their Stasi was ill. Could I replace her? Of course I could! (Twenty-five marks extra per performance.)

On the early morning train to Frankfurt, I tried to cheer myself up. Caruso had sung in *Aida* at this very same Frankfurt Opera, as a helpful colleague had reminded me just before I left. So what?

From the station I headed straight for the opera house for a quick run-through, stepped from the wings onto the stage, and looked at the huge, empty auditorium. I suddenly felt very cold. Even the orchestra pit, where eighty instruments would be accompanying me, looked like a great, black, unbridgeable abyss. Would I be able to see the conductor clearly enough to follow his baton? My new colleagues reassured me. The conductor, they said, was a good man who could enhance anybody's voice by the uncanny sensitivity of his accompaniments.

Nobody seemed worried about me as we ran through our numbers at the piano. They probably thought I was holding back to save my voice for the evening. Little did they know that I was giving my all! I spent the rest of the day gargling and doing breathing exercises, and then went to the theater early and put on my costume, which was prettier than the one in Darmstadt. That pepped me up a bit, and when I heard my cue, I strode out to the footlights convinced that a miracle would happen and a brilliant voice would issue from my mouth, as long as I opened it wide enough and breathed deeply.

The friendly audience greeted my entrance with applause for the guest performer. Courage! A short exchange of dialogue, and then my leading man and I sat down side by side in a hammock for the duet "Let's Do as the Swallows Do," rocking gently back and forth and keeping an eye on the conductor. That good man, who had never laid eyes on me before, led his orchestra through the opening bars of the famous tune and threw me an encouraging smile. But the awe-inspiring sound of those opening measures had already scared me to death, used as I was to the muted orchestral murmur of our Darmstadt conductor. No time to protest, explain, or beseech—go! I opened my mouth and sang, "I'm waiting for the happy wonder, tralala—"

The conductor stopped conducting. He leaned forward as far as he could and cupped his hand behind his ear in order to hear better. Had I started on cue or not? He thought I'd just moved my lips, because, as he told me later, not a single note had reached him.

After a few ragged chords, the orchestra gave up. In the deathly silence, a faint cheeping became audible: " . . . tralala, I've heard so much about . . . " The conductor looked at me desperately, his hand still behind his ear. I stared back just as desperately and struggled on, unaccompanied but undeterred, since no one had told me to stop.

In the meantime the audience had caught on. There was some whispering and a few guffaws. Someone in the gallery shouted, "Hey, Miss, have another go!"

On stage all was quiet, because my part in the duet was finished. Now it was my colleague's turn. But the poor man, who all this time had been holding my hand (soaking wet), according to the stage directions, didn't want to follow my example and sing without the orchestra. Silence. Gaping, black, deathly silence. Endless. A sort of rigor mortis gripped me. I could only stare at the conductor the way a rabbit stares at a cobra.

Suddenly the cobra moved, raised his baton, forced a smile to his colorless lips, and uttered the magic phrase, "*Da capo.*" Once again the orchestra plunged into the introduction, this time held firmly in check by the left hand of the wiser and sadder conductor. It is therefore possible that a few of my notes did actually reach the audience, because there was some spontaneous applause when we finished the duet. My colleague had to lift me out of the hammock so that I could take a bow. I curtseyed blindly in all directions and made my exit as fast as I could, to more applause and laughter.

Six months of my contract had elapsed, and I hadn't exactly set the town on fire with my talent. Then out of the blue came my big chance. I was offered a part in another operetta, Kunnecke's *Happy Journey*. No classic, thank God. They could overlook my singing, because the role was primarily an acting one. *Happy Journey* was a hit and earned me the first reviews I could send home.

It opened early in 1933, soon after Hitler came to power.

Until then there had been only vague rumblings and rumors. In our immediate neighborhood, no dramatic incident had occurred. Everyone went about his work and hoped for the best. My contract had another six months to run, and the managing director had already mentioned a possible renewal. But after the premiere of *Happy Journey*, the Frankfurt Playhouse offered me a two-year contract at double the salary, not as a junior member of the company but as juvenile lead. I overflowed with excitement, in spite of the hitherto unknown and quite frightening daily spectacle of Brownshirts parading with their swastika flags. Now that Hitler was actually in power, he would surely realize how complicated everything was and stop screaming. Of course he would; everybody said so. The terrible things he'd said in *Mein Kampf* were only party propaganda; everybody said so. No responsible politician would ever dream of turning thousands of good German citizens against him just because they happened to be Jews—people like Einstein and Max Reinhardt and Elisabeth Bergner. Germany surely wasn't going to try to get along without *them*?

Admittedly the new Nuremberg "racial laws" made ugly reading: everybody was required to produce his four grandparents' baptismal certificates. If you couldn't, you were declared "non-Aryan" and were eliminated from all areas of public life and held unfit to own any business, public or private. Did they really *mean* that? Of course not. It was inconceivable that any of these new "measures" would be put into effect. That was all just party politics. Propaganda. Nothing to worry about.

The following week, however, my Frankfurt contract was cancelled in a letter stating that, owing to the anticipated "reorganization," which would involve changes in the repertory and the company, the management regretted, but . . . .

So it was true after all. I read the letter sitting on the sofa in my digs. I loved my digs. Two tiny furnished rooms on the edge of town and a nice old landlady who was accustomed to theater tadpoles like me and knew how to keep up their morale before first nights by shouting kind if confused encouragement from her kitchen. "You'll do all right, my girl, I know you will—oh Lord, my cauliflower's burning—happy landings!" I knew she'd been subscribing to the *Volkische Beobachter*, the official Nazi newspaper, for the last two months, but she took to emptying her mailbox very early in the morning so I wouldn't see it. Her affection for me remained unchanged, although she knew that I didn't measure up to Goebbel's Aryan standards.

What now? No more chance for a career in Germany. Hard to swallow, because my stupid, stubborn optimism wouldn't accept it. What if the Frankfurt theater was being honest with me after all? What if it were true that they hadn't decided on next year's repertory? Nonsense. They needed a juvenile lead; the general manager had told me so himself. I might as well get used to the idea: *they didn't want me*. Was there really nothing one could do except leave the country?

My landlady stuck her unhappy face around the door to offer me a cup of coffee. She had shared my jubilations over the Frankfurt contract and she'd seen the envelope and my face that morning. Perhaps she had known what to expect. "It's really a shame," she ventured cautiously from behind her steaming coffee cup, "because you can't deny that Hitler is a good man. You bet your life he'll make Germany great again. Too bad he has this—this thing about the Jews . . . "

That night I decided it really was too bad. I'd better get it over with: give up the apartment, leave Darmstadt, leave Germany, go to England and make a new start in English. Luckily my father had sent me to England every year during the long summer vacation until I spoke the language fluently.

I put on my good blue dress and instead of going to morning rehearsal I went straight to the general manager's office, although I knew that Gustav Hartung, the man who hired me, whose avant-garde productions were admired throughout Germany, was away. As I waited outside, it occurred to me that he'd been "away" for quite a few weeks—most unusual for a man so dedicated to his theater. (He never returned. He was one of the few who "knew.")

His deputy, a kindly man, received me with friendly courtesy. I told him briefly about the letter from Frankfurt, and he stared out the window for a while before turning to me with a sigh.

"Yes," he said.

I waited, but he didn't go on. Whereupon I said I was sure that under the circumstances Darmstadt would also prefer to dispense with my services. Could I consider my contract terminated as of now? To my surprise he shook his head and replied that he had no authority to let me go. After all, I was appearing in at least four current productions, one of which, *Happy Journey*, was the theater's current hit, and he must therefore refuse my suggestion. My contract had another four months to run, and as far as he was concerned, I would be obliged to spend them in Darmstadt, working.

My second attempt to get in line with the new Germany was nipped in the bud just as fast. When I tried to replace my landlady with one who didn't subscribe to the *Volkische Beobachter*, my old one was so upset that I had to unpack again.

The following weeks went by as usual, at least outwardly: rehearsals during the day, performance at night. But I had a feeling that a certain change had taken place in the behavior of my colleagues towards me. Most of them were making a point of being extra friendly, and this made me nervous. Before, they had ignored me in the friendly fashion in which junior members of a company are meant to be ignored. Now I fancied that they spoke more loudly to me than to other people, as if they wanted to make sure it didn't go unnoticed. They never missed an opportunity to say hello and ask me how I was. A very few avoided me.

Hitler had been chancellor for only three months, but the drastic change, the radical revolution, the upheaval, that was to affect every single German—man, woman, and child—was already making itself felt. Looking back, one assumes that all Germans must have recognized from the outset what Hitler and National Socialism meant. But at the time most people—unless they were already Nazi party members, and there were only about ten thousand of those—held aloof, were undecided, looked cautiously into the future, hastily made sure their grandparents' baptismal certificates were to hand (all four of them), heaved a sigh of relief if they were, waited, read the papers, and listened to rumors.

Of course there were a few who wouldn't fall into line without protesting, or at least speaking their mind. At the Darmstadt theater they were represented loud and clear, by a few intrepid young directors and stage designers who expressed their contempt and their derision. One of them in particular, Arthur Maria Rabenalt, the young director of *Happy Journey*, loved to make fun of "dedicated" and newly surfacing party members in the company and didn't care who heard him.

The most amazing element was the appearance of those "new men." Where did they all come from? Brand-new, completely unfamiliar faces—unless you happened to remember seeing the new "Herr Direktor" delivering groceries a week or two ago or recognized the "Herr Conductor" as a former singing teacher at the local high school. Now conductor and director sported the brown SA uniform with the red and white swastika armband, their heavy black leather boots tramping loudly and insolently up and down the halls of hallowed institutions. Their orders from behind their splendid desks were easily understood by one and all: they didn't care what their underlings did as long as it was "different" from what had gone on before and, of course, as long as no non-Aryan persons were involved.

Non-Aryan. That definition became an overnight status symbol and was liberally used, though not universally understood. My mother, for instance, who had to engage a new cook at that time, told the honest Bavarian peasant woman at the end of the interview, "I must, however, draw your attention to the fact that this is a non-Aryan household." To which the good woman replied with a broad and friendly smile, "Oh, madam, it's all the same to me, Aryan or non-Aryan! The main thing is, no Jews!"

The replacement of people in leading positions began with those at the top in important political, commercial, and cultural functions and worked gradually downwards. But it was thorough. It left no business or establishment, however insignificant, untouched, and it became uglier as it went down the scale. The people who "took over" from the rightful owners were no longer those one had known locally in menial jobs, but seemed to have crawled out from underneath a stone. They all had low party registration numbers and were now being "rewarded."

The next piece we were rehearsing was called *When the Young Vine Blossoms*, a semiclassic from the middle of the last century. Director: A. M. Rabenalt. I played a young girl who makes her first entrance right at the opening of the play. This scene was staged as a kind of folk dance. The whole cast was divided into two equal groups, each of which started from one side of the stage, the actors holding hands and dancing towards the center of the footlights. The groups passed each other and danced off at the opposite exits. All this by way of "introduction to the audience."

Rehearsals had gone well, and the dress rehearsal was at last announced on the blackboard by the stage exit. This was good news to me. We were in mid-April. Ten more weeks till July 1 and the end of my contract.

The dress rehearsal went off satisfactorily. The play's mild, nineteenth-century humor and quaint sentimentality were vintage German and could not possibly offend anybody, even in these touchy times. The nervous man who was deputy general manager—no big noise had as yet officially replaced our absent former boss—watched from the stalls, very pleased, and made a little speech at the end, expressing the hope that our "heartwarming, carefree gaiety" would not be lost in tommorrow's first-night nerves.

I took off my white muslin crinoline, caught the last streetcar home, and prayed that this might be my last opening night at the theater. It wasn't likely that they would cast me in any new production. I would appear twice a week, once in my good old hit *Happy Journey* and once in this new play, and that would be it until I could pack my suitcase for good.

There was the usual run-through in the morning. On the day of a premiere, the actors would assemble in the foyer of the theater to go through their lines while finishing touches were added to the set and the lighting. The moment I entered the foyer, I knew something had happened and that it was something to do with me. Everybody was standing around in groups, talking, but when I came in, they suddenly stopped abruptly. No one said good morning. Rabenalt was nowhere to be seen.

I hung up my coat, sat down, and pretended to be busy with my script. There was a menacing, totally inexplicable, endless silence. I read one page of my script over and over again so as not to make a noise by turning the page.

At last the door opened and Rabenalt appeared. In the deathly hush, he asked me as casually as possible to follow him. I picked up my coat, feeling everybody's eyes on my every movement. He walked very fast to the general manager's office and entered without knocking. "Here she is," he said, "she's all yours!" And made for the door. But the man behind our boss's desk sat with his head in his hands and called after him, "Don't go, for goodness' sake! I need you! We've got to work something out!"

"Well, hurry up then," said Rabenalt, and fell heavily into an armchair. "Make it short. I have an opening night tonight, and now this goddam business!"

I was bidden to sit down and the unhappy deputy allowed himself a short pause before he finally addressed himself to me.

"Was your father in the last war?"

"Yes," I said, mystified.

"Thank God!" he exclaimed and sat up a bit. "Do you happen to know if he received a decoration?"

"Yes," I said. "The Iron Cross."

"What for? Do you know?"

"Because he ran a field hospital at Verdun for four years."

"Did you hear that?" said the deputy, filled with sudden enthusiasm, to Rabenalt. "That might make a difference, don't you think?"

"It might," said Rabenalt, and they both looked at me as if I were the one who had run the Verdun field hospital.

"Would you mind telling me . . . " I began.

They told me. That morning they had received a memo from the commander of the local Storm Troops saying he had just been informed that a new play was to open that night at the State Theater in which an actress of non-Aryan extraction would appear. This was a contravention of the order that such persons were permitted to appear only in old productions in which they could not be replaced by Aryan performers. A platoon of twenty-five Storm Troopers would therefore occupy the front row of the stalls that evening. At my entrance they would demonstrate "in an appropriate manner" and reserve the right to take "further measures."

For the last three months such "spontaneous" demonstrations had been nothing new in the German theater. We had heard of several similar outbursts of patriotic indignation throughout Germany, though so far nothing of the sort had happened at Darmstadt. If a local Storm Troop commander or his group leader didn't like a play or its author, or if actors were suspected of "cultural Bolshevism" or had been members of the Communist party or even friends of members (although until three months ago the Communist party had been a perfectly legal organization), the commander would send a detachment of Brownshirts to demonstrate. This could mean a variety of things: they might throw rotten eggs, or interrupt the performance, or jump onto the stage, beat up the actors and haul the particular target of the evening off into "protective custody." "Protective custody" was the euphemistic name for that new institution—new to Germany, at least—the concentration camp. There, according to the newspapers, "unreliable" people would be "protected" from the legitimate wrath of their fellow citizens.

Even in its mildest form, such an evening at the theater was pretty frightening for the audience, not to mention the actors. Now I understood my reception in the foyer. They all knew.

The deputy manager sprang to life and issued orders into the telephone. He demanded to speak immediately to the chief of the local Storm Troopers, as he had vital information concerning tonight's demonstration at the theater. The Nazi boss, however, was nowhere to be found. Word was left for him at his office, at his home, all over town, to please contact the theater immediately.

Seconds later the telephone did indeed ring and the manager jumped, but it was only the box-office lady reporting that twenty-five seats in the front row had been requisitioned by the Storm Troopers, which meant reseating twenty-five ordinary ticketholders. Should she? Yes, she should. There was nothing else to be done for the moment. I was sent to my dressing room, where I was to wait.

The simplest course would have been to replace me, but I had no understudy and Rabenalt resolutely refused to start rehearsing somebody else. The question was, were the actors willing to go through with the opening under these conditions or would they refuse and demand that the premiere be postponed until a replacement could be found? Insults, rotten eggs, a possible beating up, on top of the usual first-night jitters—wasn't it too much to ask?

I sat in my silent dressing room and tried to keep calm. The fact that within a few hours I might be taken off into "protective custody" did not enter my mind. Things like that just didn't happen to me!

My father's decoration. I remembered having read somewhere that non-Aryans who had served at the front in World War I could claim "special privileges." I also remembered dimly having once seen the box containing the cross and its ribbon. Only once. He never wore it. No one wore medals in the Weimar Republic. My father rarely spoke about his war experiences, but I knew that they had been as harrowing as those of millions of others. All the same, he had come back. Throughout my school days, the "free tuition inspector" used to show up in our classroom every few months. At the command "All war orphans please stand up," seven out of twenty children would rise to their feet, self-conscious and resentful, all of them shabbily dressed and peaked. Seven out of twenty . . . .

Hours went by, and I was still sitting in my dressing room. My dresser came in, bringing sandwiches and coffee. No, she hadn't heard anything new. Yes, they'd had the run-through with the prompter reading my part. I was to stay here until further notice. Did I want anything? I wanted a whole lot of things, but nothing that friendly old soul could provide. I pushed a couple of chairs together, lay down, and fell asleep.

Toward evening the silent theater started to wake up. I heard footsteps and colleagues' voices in the halls. At last

my door opened and Rabenalt came in. He looked ex-
hausted. "Well," he said, "there's nothing else to do but
go through with it. The others are willing to take the risk.
What about you?"

I nodded.

"Good. We haven't been able to reach the Storm
Troopers' commander, but we're still trying. There's still
plenty of time before the curtain goes up. So get
ready—and good luck!"

He left. I began to lay out my makeup in my corner of
the room. Two other actresses, playing minor roles,
appeared and nodded to me. There was none of the hectic
chatter of an opening night. Both of them remained grimly
silent.

As I began to put on my makeup, I suddenly lost my
nerve. From one minute to the next. I stared into the mirror, scared and furious with myself for having said yes so
thoughtlessly. Why, in God's name? And for whom? I
shot dirty looks at the other two, as if it had been their
fault. If only somebody would come and tell us something!

Nobody came. Only the call boy, making his rounds,
calling the hour until curtain time, then the half hour, and
finally fifteen minutes. There wasn't a sound to be heard
on our floor.

We had finished our makeup, and the old dresser came
to help us into our crinolines. "No news," she snapped as
she came in, cutting off any further conversation.

"Five minutes!" shouted the call boy outside the door,
and we trooped downstairs.

On stage they were all crowding around Rabenalt, who
was giving them a last-minute pep talk. He looked up when
he saw me, tried to smile, and continued, "As I was saying, it's a good thing you all make your entrance together

holding hands. I don't think anything will happen as long as Frau Menz is on stage." (Menz was our leading lady.) "Everybody loves her. Honestly, I don't think there'll be any violence. Be prepared for catcalls and whistling and that sort of thing and try to carry on as if nothing had happened. And . . . er . . . if they throw things, try to ignore it and keep going. Only if they actually jump on stage—then I think it would be better if you'd all stop. I've given instructions for the fire curtain to be rung down immediately."

The leading man interrupted. "Are you sure they're actually in the house?"

Rabenalt nodded. "They got here fifteen minutes ago. Lined up outside and filed in in double ranks. Take a look! You can't miss them. Front row center."

The actor went and looked through the peephole into the house. He came back without a word.

At that moment, the houselights dimmed and the call boy shouted, "Places, please." No more time for anybody to question or argue. We took our places in the wings on either side of the stage, hand in hand, ready to make our entrance, while the orchestra struck up a short introduction.

And then it happened. The actress whose right hand I was to hold, a woman in her late twenties who played one of the leads, pulled her hand free and faced me, her eyes desperate. "You don't really count," she said as loud as she dared, "you're only a child, but as far as most of the Jews I've met in my life are concerned, all I can say is—" and she spat with great precision on the floor between us.

"For God's sake, Dorothea!" hissed the actor next to her, aghast.

But she turned once more to me. "Enough's enough,"

she said, trembling. "I just want to make it clear where I stand."

The orchestra stopped, and a loud rushing noise told us that the curtain was going up. In a flash the stage was bathed in brilliant sunshine, and the first daisy chain of actors, Frau Menz in the middle, danced toward us, laughing gaily. Dorothea grabbed my hand—she grabbed my hand!—and we too, with joyous guffaws, began to skip in the direction of the footlights. As I was propelled speedily forward, my heart was pounding like a kettledrum. Any minute now . . . would they? . . . now! Here was the crucial moment: the footlights! Now? Onwards, halfway across—I almost flew . . . ten more steps and I would be able to disappear into the wings on the other side . . . still nothing . . . three more steps . . . made it! There was our goal, our deliverance, our haven: the stage manager's little stool! (With the poor man standing next to it, his prompt script, his glasses, and both hands convulsively clutched to his stomach.)

Breathless and sweating we collected ourselves in the darkness of the wings while the action continued onstage between blessed Frau Menz and a couple of minor actors. In their excitement nobody noticed that I was right among them, one of them, so to speak. Why had nothing happened? Was our entrance too fast or were there too many people onstage at the same time? Was it all over or was it still to come?

At that moment Rabenalt joined us. He had been sitting in the stage box physically sick with anxiety, so he said, and had rushed backstage through the secret connecting door. He could hardly speak, as he was holding up his hands in biblical gesture of rejoicing. "They're gone!" he whispered hoarsely. "They all got up during the overture

and left! I saw somebody in uniform arrive and hand a
message to the one nearest the exit. After that, they just
got up and filed out. Information! Didn't you know?''

No. No one had known. Everyone had aged a few years
in the course of that short dance across the stage. Our
"heartwarming, carefree gaiety" was gone. We drooped.

The evening dragged to its close. The audience was
obviously disturbed, too. What was the meaning of the
conspicuous exit of all those uniforms in the front row?
Leaden silence hung over the performance. When the curtain fell, there was barely polite applause, followed by a
rush towards the exit.

Next morning, I received a letter from the deputy
manager: my father's Iron Cross had done it. The Storm
Troops' commander had received the message in the nick
of time. He, too, had spent several unforgettable years in
the trenches at Verdun.

But the writing on the wall stood out in capital letters as
far as I was concerned. Get out, it said. Get out of Darmstadt. Get out of Germany. At once! The only question
was where to go.

The day I returned to Berlin, my father and mother and
I sat up late into the night, arguing. Paris was their choice,
because my sister Irene had been there for a month
already, trying to get a foothold somehow. London was
mine. But not my father's. "You're going to join Irene in
Paris," he said. "You're still a child; you're too young to
live alone in a foreign country. There's no more to be
said."

At that point the "child" was just going through the ups
and downs of her first love affair: Rolf Gérard, painter
and medical student. "Aryan." Our love affair was
already one year old. I had met him in a cafe on the Kur-

fürstendamm in Berlin shortly before my high school finals. I was sitting alone at a table looking at my wristwatch, waiting for a girl friend. So was he. We had both been stood up and started ogling each other instead. He joined me forthwith at my table, we drank a coffee together, went for a long, long walk, and fell passionately in love. I was seventeen, he was twenty-three. When I left for Darmstadt a few months later, he contrived to inscribe himself at the University of Heidelberg, an hour's train journey away. We visited each other as often as we could afford it, wrote hundreds of letters, and talked on the telephone. When I broke it to him tht I was going to emigrate to Paris, he said, after a moment of contemplation, that strangely enough he had planned to go there too, to continue his studies at the Sorbonne. At Heidelberg University, he had been forced to attend a certain number of lectures on Nazi ideology every week, without which he wouldn't have been eligible to take his exams. ID cards were stamped at the entrance to the building, to prevent cheating. Rolf had shown up at the first session as required, but from then on, as soon as he had had his card stamped, he jumped out of the window to avoid sitting through the lecture. The third time he sprained his ankle.

That did it. There was only one solution for both of us: Paris.

THE PRICE OF MY SOUL
by Bernadette Devlin

Bernadette Devlin has had police both clear the way for her as a Member of Parliament—at twenty-one she was the youngest M.P. since Pitt—and thwart her as a protester. In The Price of My Soul *she disavows having written an autobiography or a political manifesto, but claims instead to have attempted "to explain how the complex of economic, social, and political problems of Northern Ireland threw up the phenomenon of Bernadette Devlin." In using the word "phenomenon" she has not intended to usurp for herself a unique, historical role. Indeed, she asserts that she is only one among hundreds of her generation born to an unjust system but not prepared to grow old in it.*

She explained that the title of her book has a family significance. Her dead mother had planned to write her autobiography using this title. Because she more than anyone else was responsible for her daughter's attitude toward life and its misery, Bernadette felt it was fitting to use the intended title of the other autobiography that would never now be written.

Bernadette Devlin writes that "The Price of My Soul" refers not to the price for which she would sell out but rather to the price we all must pay to preserve our integrity. She points out that "To gain that which is worth having, it may be necessary to lose everything else."

THE Civil Rights Association had been in existence for two years, during which time it had been doing ordinary constitutional things like writing to Members of Parliament, and getting nowhere by these methods. There was only one thing to do, they decided, and that was to take the movement to the people, so on August 24, 1968, they organized a civil-rights march from Coalisland to Dungannon, a distance of some three miles. I read about it in a newspaper and thought to myself, Civil-rights march! Excellent idea! It's about time somebody did something about the situation in Northern Ireland. And I set off to join it with my young brother and friend.

At Coalisland there were masses of people milling around, selling civil-rights rosettes, eating oranges, and generally behaving as if they were at a carnival. The march was supposed to start at six o'clock on this bright August evening, but of course it started late, and it wasn't until about seven o'clock that we trudged off up the road led by a band of children playing accordions. We had been told this was a nonsectarian, nonpolitical march—for all that the demands we were making were political. Nevertheless politically minded young people had turned up with banners of their associations—the Young Liberals, the Young Socialists, and so on—but they weren't allowed to carry them. The marchers were interspersed with various bands, playing "Who Fears to Speak of '98" and "Faith of Our Fathers." "Faith of Our Fathers" is a Catholic hymn which has been degraded by frequent playing at Nationalist gatherings and is one song I hate to hear at a political meeting, because it betrays the old mentality that equates Irish and Catholic. But we had a bash at "Faith of Our Fathers" anyway: so much for nonsectarian. We had stewards marshalling up who thought we were in the army, and kept singing out, "Pick up your feet! March in fours! One, two; one, two!" and everyone was just roaring at them. It was an event. It was the first civil-rights demonstration Northern Ireland had ever seen, and we all jogged along happily eating oranges and smoking cigarettes, and people came out of their houses to join the fun. Marchers were dropping off at every pub on the way, and the whole thing had a sort of good-natured, holiday atmosphere, with the drunk men lolloping in and out of this supposedly serious demonstration.

Then we got to Dungannon, and the carnival feeling faltered. There was a police cordon across the road. We weren't going to be allowed into the town. At first the marchers only got half-heartedly annoyed, and some of them were roaring across on first-name terms to policemen they knew, but when the officer in charge came over and said that in the interests of the peace the march was being rerouted into the Catholic section of Dungannon, the whole atmosphere changed. Most of the people on the march hadn't really thought about civil rights: they had come, with a sort of friendly curiosity, to hear something. I do believe that then for the first time it dawned on people that Northern Ireland was a series of Catholic and Protestant ghettos. The meeting got very angry, though it was still a passive anger, with very little pushing and shoving of the police. Some men were calling out that we should force our way through, and the lines of the march were breaking formation and crowding up to the police. Everyone forgot about the accordion-playing children, about to be squashed between the opposing forces. Then my young brother grabbed a megaphone and bellowed through it: would the drunk men get out of the march, would the women take the children out of the march and get out of the way themselves. People made a move to do as he said until they realized the orders came from a fifteen-year-old boy, when they said, "My God, what's he talking about? You'd think there was going to be trouble." So John himself started leading the children to safety.

Meanwhile the leaders of the Civil Rights Association, which had called the march, were organizing a meeting there on the spot, in front of the police cordon. A lorry was brought up as a platform, and chairs and a microphone were put on the back of it, and the organizers announced that we weren't going to force our way into Dungannon because this was a nonviolent march. They were beginning to lose their hold on the marchers, though. People shouted, "What's the point of saying we'll get civil rights when you let them stop us having *this* civil right?" Gerry Fitt, the Republican Labour Member at Westminister for Belfast West, tried to match the feeling of the meeting, which was becoming more angry and rowdy by the minute. "If one of those black bastards on the Northern Ireland Gestapo puts a hand on any man here, I'll lead you through!" he stormed. Just at that moment a policeman with a big blackthorn stick struck a man, and the crowd literally cheered, dragged Gerry off the platform, and pushed him up to the front to keep his promise. Gerry fought his way back to the platform, scrambled up, and said, "Remember, there are women and children amongst us." Betty Sinclair, chairman and leading light of the Civil Rights Association in those days, got up, fearing the movement would be discredited if a fight broke out. "This is a nonpolitical, peaceful demonstration. Anyone who wants to fight should get out and join the IRA," she said. And the crowd roared back, "Where do we join?" Betty then realized that without any forethought at all she had organized a march in Coalisland, a town that was 90 percent Republican; she had brought them out; they had been frustrated by the police; and she had nothing constructive to offer them. She decided that the only thing she could safely do was wind up the meeting. "We'll end the meeting now, ladies and gentlemen," she said. "and before we go, we'll sing the civil-rights anthem." Nobody had heard of civil rights before, never mind the civil-rights anthem, so she went on, "The civil-rights anthem, 'We Shall Overcome.' " Like Sir Malcolm Sargent at the Promenade Concerts, she raised her arms and started, "We shall overcome . . . ," and everbody else started, "A nation once again . . . " By the time we'd got to the end of the first verse of our anthem, Betty and all her friends had scuttled into the lorry and driven off, leaving the population of Coalisland outside the town of Dungannon.

After that we sat down in big circles all over the road and sang rebel songs till midnight. There were one or two scuffles in Dungannon in which individuals who went into town were beaten up by angry Unionists, but that was all. The police were very good-natured. They really didn't know what to do about us. It was a situation they'd never faced before, so they left us there to sing till we were tired, and then we all went home. It wasn't a fiasco precisely, that first march: at least it wakened people up a bit, but it seemed to have no echo in the weeks that followed and everybody was prepared to forget about it. I went back to the pub and thought about it and wondered when the next march would be held. I felt very cynical about the performance of the politicians and organizers: it was hilarious to see how out of touch they were with the people they supposedly represented. They thought they could come down, make big speeches, and be listened to respectfully, but when the people all got out together, they had turned round and said in effect to the politicians, "Clear off, you don't even *think* the way we think." And that's exactly what the politicians did: they cleared off.

In spite of their "civil-rights" label, the politicians had demanded *Catholic* equality and majority rule for *Catholic* areas. People like myself had not come to support such demands. We had come because we wanted to be involved—we were not quite sure in what. We knew something was wrong with a society where the rate of unemployment rarely fell below 10 per cent, where half the houses lacked at least one basic amenity. The politicians tried to tell us it was a nonpolitical demonstration; but though our politics were crude in those days, we were more politically aware than "the leaders" in that we refused to accept their logic that the problems could be seen in terms of Catholic versus Protestant.

Our system is one in which the basic divide is thought to be along religious lines, in which it is quite rational for a man to believe he is sentenced to unemployment for the crime of being a Catholic. But he is not. He is sentenced to unemployment because there are not enough jobs, and there are not enough jobs because investment is made on grounds of profit, not on grounds of people's needs. The crowd at that first-ever civil-rights march was interested in people's needs.

I also thought about the strength of feeling the march had shown, the amount of frustration people felt, and their readiness to release this frustration in wanton violence. But mainly I was just glad I'd seen people standing there outside Dungannon saying all the things they had never dared to say in the pub. People were coming into the pub now and saying quietly, "Were you on the march? Wasn't it great?"

So when the next march, to be held in Londonderry on

October 5, was announced, I welcomed it. Londonderry, traditionally called simply Derry, is the flash point of Northern Ireland. Because of the Siege of Londonderry in 1689—when the citizens inside the walls held out against the Catholic besiegers for 105 days before help came—it has enormous emotional value as a symbol to the Protestants, but it also has among the worst records in housing, employment, and political manipulation in the whole country. It is a place where passions don't need much to be aroused, and the Minister of Home Affairs, Mr. William Craig, banned the march. The reaction to the ban showed how far people's resignation had begun to crack. In the past when things were banned, you complained, you sulked, and you went home. More people turned up to the Derry march because it was banned than would have come if the government had done nothing about it. The silence was beginning to be broken.

I went to Derry on October 5 and found there an atmosphere that the city had never had before. Ordinarily Derry is a dead city: about one in five of the men is unemployed and the whole feeling of the place is depressed. But it was electric that day. You could see it on people's faces—excitement, or alarm, or anger. Derry was alive. My friends and I didn't know where the march was beginning, and we were afraid to ask, in case we asked the wrong person and got clobbered for our trouble. But we found it in the end and started off.

We hadn't got more than a couple of hundred yards up the street when we were stopped by masses of police. There were a few scuffles. The police took our banners away and knocked a few people over the head . . . .

I had been watching the police and I'd seen them filter down both sides of the march, so that now they encircled us. When we turned to go back down the street and re-form, we found we were trapped, There were policemen to the right and the left, to the fore and the aft, and they just moved in on all four sides, with truncheons and heels and boots, and beat everybody off the street. Then the water cannons came out and hosed the streets. Quite deliberately they hosed in upstairs windows and shop fronts, and they went right across Craigavon Bridge, hosing all the onlookers. The police just went mad.

Derry was on every newspaper in Ireland, every newspaper in Britain. It was being flashed on every television screen in the world. Telefis Eireann (the Southern Ireland television network) had a smart cameraman who filmed the whole thing, sold the film to every company who could get their hands on it, and gave Harold Wilson a private showing. And Ireland was up in arms: you can slowly crush the Irish, you can take the ground from under their feet and they won't notice they're sinking down; but if you hit them, they will hit back. So the Unionist government did the civil-rights movement a favor. They gave it life in one day. Without the police, it would have taken much longer to get off the ground.

While everyone was running madly around me, I was standing still—not because I hadn't panicked, but because panic had a different effect on me. I was standing almost paralyzed, watching the expressions on the faces of the police. Arms and legs were flying everywhere, but what horrified me was the evil delight the police were showing as they beat people down, then beat them again to prevent them from getting up, then trailed them up and threw them on for somebody else to give them a thrashing. It was as though they had been waiting to do it for fifty years. Perhaps because I was the only person who wasn't running, I wasn't touched at all, but as I was standing there a young fellow came up, grabbed me by the arm, and said, "For Christ's sake, move!" Just as he pushed me in front of him, which left him standing where I had been, a policeman clobbered him, splitting his head down the side. Even though the blood was pouring down his face, the police weren't prepared to leave him alone: they made him run the gauntlet, until we got him out beyond the cordon and took him into a barber's shop. When he was roughly patched up, we brought him to Altnagelvin Hospital for stitches, and later when we went back to collect him, we were asked, "Was he one of those people at the demonstration?"

"We don't really know," I said. "He was hit by something, anyway, and brought in here to get stitched."

"Well, if he was one of those demonstrators, he didn't get hit hard enough." Such was the impartial attitude of those ministering to the sick. They wouldn't tell us who he was, where he was, or how he was, and having discovered the color of the skin of Altnagelvin Hospital, we decided the sooner we got out of there the better.

After that I walked into a pub, literally shaking, and swallowed one double whiskey neat without tasting it. So began my civil-rights commitment and my whiskey drinking.

AN AUTOBIOGRAPHY
The Story of My Experiments with Truth
by Mohandas K. Gandhi

Viewers of newsreels in the Thirties and Forties became familiar with pictures of a frail Hindu dressed in loincloth and shawl, smiling and determined. This was Mahatama Gandhi of whom Einstein wrote in 1944: "Generations to come, it may be, will scarcely believe that such a one as this ever in flesh and blood walked upon this earth." The title "Mahatama" (Great Soul) by which he had come to be known reflected his high personal prestige, and made it possible for him to exact political concessions from the British by threatening to fast unto death. Gandhi's program included a free, united India, revival of cottage industries, and the abolition of untouchability. His methods of non-violent civil disobedience were adopted by protagonists of civil rights in the United States and by many protest movements throughout the world.

As a child, Mohandas Gandhi was quiet, shy, retiring. He was perhaps unusually serious and passive. B. R. Nanda, one of his biographers, points out, however, that he had a burning passion for self-improvement. This ideal of self-improvement he tried to impose on his girl-wife, Kasturbai.

Today in India an estimated 95 per cent of marriages are still arranged. This is true of all classes. Girls are usually 18, boys usually over 21. Both sexes have the opportunity to object to the particular person chosen. (I have a friend whose nephew five times has turned down the young woman selected.) It would be difficult, if not impossible, to convince most Indians that the American way of marrying is better.

IT is my painful duty to have to record here my marriage at the age of thirteen. As I see the youngsters of the same age about me who are under my care, and think of my own marriage, I am inclined to pity myself and to congratulate them on having escaped my lot. I can see no moral argument in support of such a preposterously early marriage.

Let the reader make no mistake. I was married, not betrothed. For in Kathiwad there are two distinct rites —betrothal and marriage. Betrothal is a preliminary promise on the part of the parents of the boy and the girl to join them in marriage, and it is not inviolable. The death of the boy entails no widowhood on the girl. It is an agreement purely between the parents, and the children have no concern with it. Often they are not even informed of it. It appears that I was betrothed thrice, though without my knowledge. I was told that two girls chosen for me had died in turn, and therefore I infer that I was betrothed three times. I have a faint recollection, however, that the third betrothal took place in my seventh year. But I do not recollect having been informed about it. In the present chapter I am talking about my marriage, of which I have the clearest recollection.

It will be remembered that we were three brothers. The first was already married. The elders decided to marry my second brother, who was two or three years my senior, a cousin, possibly a year older, and me, all at the same time. In doing so there was no thought of our welfare, much less our wishes. It was purely a question of their own convenience and economy.

Marriage among Hindus is no simple matter. The parents of the bride and the bridegroom often bring themselves to ruin over it. They waste their substance, they waste their time. Months are taken up over the preparations—in making clothes and ornaments and in preparing budgets for dinners. Each tried to outdo the other in the number and variety of courses to be prepared. Women, whether they have a voice or no, sing themselves hoarse, even get ill, and disturb the peace of their neighbours. These in their turn quietly put up with all the turmoil and bustle, all the dirt and filth, representing the remains of the feasts, because they know that a time will come when they also will be behaving in the same manner.

It would be better, thought my elders, to have all this bother over at one and the same time. Less expense and greater *eclat*. For money could be freely spent if it had only to be spent once instead of thrice. My father and my uncle were both old, and we were the last children they had to marry. It is likely that they wanted to have the last best time of their lives. In view of all these considerations, a triple wedding was decided upon, and as I have said before, months were taken up in preparation for it.

It was only through these preparations that we got warning of the coming event. I do not think it meant to me anything more than the prospect of good clothes to wear, drum beating, marriage processions, rich dinners and a strange girl to play with. The carnal desire came later. I propose to draw the curtain over my shame, except for a few details worth recording. To these I shall come later. But even they have little to do with the central idea I have kept before me in writing this story.

So my brother and I were both taken to Porbandar from Rajkot. There are some amusing details of the preliminaries to the final drama—*e.g.* smearing our bodies all over with turmeric paste—but I must omit them.

My father was a Diwan, but nevertheless a servant, and all the more so because he was in favour with the Thakore

Saheb. The latter would not let him go until the
last moment. And when he did so, he ordered for my
father special stage coaches, reducing the journey by two
days. But the fates had willed otherwise. Porbandar is 120
miles from Rajkot—a cart journey of five days. My father
did the distance in three, but the coach toppled over in the
third stage, and he sustained severe injuries. He arrived
bandaged all over. Both his and our interest in the coming
event was half destroyed, but the ceremony had to be gone
through. For how could the marriage dates be changed?
However, I forgot my grief over my father's injuries in the
childish amusement of the wedding.

I was devoted to my parents. But no less was I devoted
to the passions that flesh is heir to. I had yet to learn that
all happiness and pleasure should be sacrificed in devoted
service to my parents. And yet, as though by way of
punishment for my desire for pleasures, an incident happened, which has ever since rankled in my mind and which
I will relate later. Nishkulanand sings: "Renunciation of
objects, without the renunciation of desires, is short-lived,
however hard you may try." Whenever I sing this song or
hear it sung, this bitter untoward incident rushes to my
memory and fills me with shame.

My father put on a brave face in spite of his injuries, and
took full part in the wedding. As I think of it, I can even
today call before my mind's eye the places where he sat as
he went through the different details of the ceremony. Little did I dream then that one day I should severely criticize
my father for having married me as a child. Everything on
that day seemed to me right and proper and pleasing.
There was also my own eagerness to get married. And as
everything that my father did then struck me as beyond
reproach, the recollection of those things is fresh in my

memory. I can picture to myself, even today, how we sat on our wedding dais, how we performed the *Saptapadi*[1], how we, the newly wedded husband and wife, put the sweet *Kansar*[2] into each other's mouth, and how we began to live together. And oh! that first night. Two innocent children all unwittingly hurled themselves into the ocean of life. My brother's wife had thoroughly coached me about my behaviour on the first night. I do not know who had coached my wife. I have never asked her about it, nor am I inclined to do so now. The reader may be sure that we were too nervous to face each other. We were certainly too shy. How was I to talk to her, and what was I to say? The coaching could not carry me far. But no coaching is really necessary in such matters. The impressions of the former birth are potent enough to make all coaching superfluous. We gradually began to know each other, and to speak freely together. We were the same age. But I took no time in assuming the authority of a husband.

About the time of my marriage, little pamphlets costing a *pice*, or a *pie* (I now forget how much), used to be issued, in which conjugal love, thrift, child marriages, and other such subjects were discussed. Whenever I came across any of these, I used to go through them cover to cover, and it was a habit with me to forget what I did not like, and to carry out in practice whatever I liked. Lifelong faithfulness to the wife, inculcated in these booklets as the duty of the husband, remained permanently imprinted on my heart. Furthermore, the passion for truth was innate in me, and to be false to her was therefore out of the question. And then there was very little chance of my being faithless at that tender age.

But the lesson of faithfulness had also an untoward

effect. "If I should be pledged to be faithful to my wife, she also should be pledged to be faithful to me," I said to myself. The thought made me a jealous husband. Her duty was easily converted into my right to exact faithfulness from her, and if it had to be exacted, I should be watchfully tenacious of the right. I had absolutely no reason to suspect my wife's fidelity, but jealousy does not wait for reasons. I must needs be for ever on the look-out regarding her movements, and therefore she could not go anywhere without my permission. This sowed the seeds of a bitter quarrel between us. The restraint was virtually a sort of imprisonment. And Kasturbai was not the girl to brook any such thing. She made it a point to go out whenever and wherever she liked. More restraint on my part resulted in more liberty being taken by her, and in my getting more and more cross. Refusal to speak to one another thus became the order of the day with us, married children. I think it was quite innocent of Kasturbai to have taken those liberties with my restrictions. How could a guileless girl brook any restraint on going to the temple or on going on visits to friends? If I had the right to impose restrictions on her, had not she also a similar right? All this is clear to me today. But at that time I had to make good my authority as a husband!

Let not the reader think, however, that ours was a life of unrelieved bitterness. For my severities were all based on love. I wanted to *make* my wife an ideal wife. My ambition was to *make* her live a pure life, learn what I learnt, and identify her life and thought with mine.

I do not know whether Kasturbai had any such ambition. She was illiterate. By nature she was simple, independent, persevering and, with me at least, reticent. She was not impatient of her ignorance and I do not recollect my studies having ever spurred her to go in for a similar adventure. I fancy, therefore, that my ambition was all one-sided. My passion was entirely centered on one woman, and I wanted it to be reciprocated. But even if there were no reciprocity, it could not be all unrelieved misery because there was active love on one side at least.

I must say I was passionately fond of her. Even at school I used to think of her, and the thought of nightfall and our subsequent meeting was ever haunting me. Separation was unbearable. I used to keep her awake till late in the night with my idle talk. If with this devouring passion there had not been in me a burning attachment to duty, I should either have fallen a prey to disease and premature death, or have sunk into a burdensome existence. But the appointed tasks had to be gone through every morning, and lying to anyone was out of the question. It was this last thing that saved me from many a pitfall.

I have already said that Kasturbai was illiterate. I was very anxious to teach her, but lustful love left me no time. For one thing the teaching had to be done against her will, and that too at night. I dared not meet her in the presence of the elders, much less talk to her. Kathiawad had then, and to a certain extent has even today, its own peculiar, useless and barbarous *Purdah*. Circumstances were thus unfavourable. I must therefore confess that most of my efforts to instruct Kasturbai in our youth were unsuccessful. And when I awoke from that sleep of lust, I had already launched forth into public life, which did not leave me much spare time. I failed likewise to instruct her through private tutors. As a result Kasturbai can now with difficulty write simple letters and understand simple Gujarati. I am sure that, had my love for her been absolutely untainted with lust, she would be a learned lady today; for

I could then have conquered her dislike for studies. I know that nothing is impossible for pure love.

---

1. *Saptapadi* are seven steps a Hindu bride and bridegroom walk together, making at the same time promises of mutual fidelity and devotion, after which the marriage becomes irrevocable.

2. *Kansar* is a preparation of wheat which the pair partake of together after the completion of the ceremony.

MARY
by Mary E. McBane

*The most significant person in Mary McBane's early life
was her Aunt Jo. Jo lived with the McBanes—Rufus,
Mary's father, was her brother—for several years in the
Wildwood black community in Durham County, North
Carolina. Eventually, however, Mary's mother, Nonnie,
who did not like her sister-in-law, succeeded in getting rid
of her.*

*From her Aunt Jo, Mary received love, encouragement,
inspiration. Her mother, on the other hand, showed her
daughter only coldness; Mary never felt that she could
please her mother.*

*An early traumatic experience would come back to
bother Mary from time to time. At the age of five she
wakened one rainy night needing to go to the bathroom, an
outside contrivance. Frightened to go outdoors in the dark
she called to her mother. Her mother, annoyed, forced the
child to go alone in the rain, thus subjecting her to a terri-
fying experience that she was never able to understand. In
a sense, the occurrence came to symbolize Nonnie's
attitude toward her.*

*In her autobiography Mary describes her aunt: "... a
tall, slim lady. She held herself very straight. She had long,
black hair that hung to her waist when she let it
down .... She was ivory-colored and had a sharp nose.
She also had a sharp tongue and would cuss if you made
her mad."*

*Mary McBane grew up wanting to please her mother and
aunt. That today she has a doctorate from the University*

*of North Carolina and is on the faculty of the University of
Wisconsin (Milwaukee) would be more likely to please her
aunt than her mother.*

AUNT Jo had strange, big-city ways: she smoked cigarettes on the sly, used rouge, introduced strange cuisine in
the household, and put unsuitable notions in my head.
Getting rid of her was a long-drawn out campaign, but
Nonnie did it—Jo moved to town and shared rooms with
two maiden sisters.

When she left, the light went out for me. I never knew
again the warmth, feeling, and loving concern that Aunt
Jo had shown me during those years. There was no one to
whisper to me about the marvelous things that I was going
to accomplish or tell me that I was meant for really great
things in life: dancer, pianist, college student. But the
damage had been done. In her quiet, determined way,
Aunt Jo had planted the seeds so deep that no one could
ever uproot them.

Nevertheless, having maneuvered Jo out of the house,
Nonnie set herself the task of eradicating those unsuitable
notions from her daughter's head. They were nothing but
foolishness and would lead Mary to nothing but trouble.
She was sorry that Ruf had let Jo stay that long, bringing
those Northern ideas and ways that she had learned from
rich people into her home. Anything associated with Jo's
notions—my being a pianist, an intellectual—she would
attack; anything not done properly in the house she would
severely condemn.

On my part, I was hardheaded and stubborn. And in
spite of all the fussing, I would not change. I brought a
book home every day and read it between the time I got
home and the time I went to bed. The okra still burned, the

chicken burned and the bread burned. Not really bad, just spots here and there, and I became adept at scraping the burned places off and putting the food back into the frying pan to brown a little more. The flour for the gravy had to be attended to every minute or it would burn so bad I'd have to throw it out and start all over, and Nonnie could not tolerate whitish gravy. So, somewhere down the line I learned about paprika, and for a while produced the reddest, spiciest gravy you ever saw. But Nonnie got wise to that—I probably put in so much that she could taste it—and I learned to cook the flour a little, then use paprika a little, not so you'd notice, but enough to speed the browning time up a bit.

If my cooking was bad, my housekeeping was worse. It would take me half the night to wash the supper dishes, for if the book I was reading was a good one, I'd read a few pages, then go wash a dish or two, then go back and read a few more. The beds got "spreaded up," not made; I took the attitude: What's the difference? You're only going to sleep in them again, anyway. And as Nonnie's fussing became sharper and the negative things she said about me got worse, I hurried even more to finish the chores and get to what I really liked. Maybe I *would* go crazy and wind up in Goldsboro. Maybe I *was* an "odd" child. But I would read that book. I know now that subconsciously I was resisting her in the only way I knew how, not by saying anything but just by not doing what she valued and wanted me to value.

One Sunday morning I had just come in from Sunday school and was sitting in the kitchen, leaning back in a straight chair propped against the wall. It was a warm day; I was slightly sweaty from walking in the heat. I lost my balance and the chair I was sitting in tipped to the left. I fell in the same direction; my head and the knob on the back of the chair hit the window, cracking the pane.

"See what you done!" Nonnie said. "I told you and told you about leaning back in that chair." I was mortified. She had told me before, but what stunned me was the rage and triumph I heard in her voice.

"I'm going to make your daddy whip you. That's what you need. A good whipping! You're getting beside yourself!"

I was too stunned to answer. Aunt Jo was gone, and though my father was sick and irritable most of the time, he let me help him in the little store that he had set up near the house, and asked me to do little things for him—so I knew he liked me. Now she wanted him to turn against me too.

I thought that there was a magical line that separated children from grown people, that when you reached a certain age you automatically stopped acting "childish"—no longer had such traits, as jealousy, spitefulness, meanness—and began acting grown, which was the way the church taught. Those who didn't act that way were sinners. The church taught: "Children, obey your parents, for this is right" and "Honor thy father and mother that thy days may be long upon the land which the Lord thy God giveth thee"; and the minister preached of the Prodigal Son, who took his portion and went and wasted it, but when he came back his father welcomed him with a big feast. In the first grade, their mother loved Dick and Jane, and in the magazines that I read parents loved and cared for their children. So if my mother didn't like and didn't care for me and always spoke to me harshly, she must have a good reason.

I thought and thought as to what the matter was

—maybe she knew what had happened to me that night in the rain when I was five years old. I didn't, for I could never clearly remember the part where I fell down. I could remember starting out in the rain and going to the barn and running back to bed, but the part where I was scream- ing and fell down was cloudy to me and I never could remember. Or maybe my mother knew about my secret longings and my erotic fantasies, though I kept them hid- den and never showed any signs of interest in boys.

But today something snapped. Something inside said, No.

"Just wait until he comes to the house. I'm going to make him whip you," she said again.

I wanted to cry, I'm a woman now, I'm not supposed to get any more whippings. But I said nothing.

I wondered about the triumphant tone that I heard in my mother's voice and then realized that it was because at last she could confront my father with something damaging about me. He and Jesse had been bitter enemies for a long time, but my mother liked Jesse, for he had been her firstborn; so it must have been galling to her to have my father talk to him mean and try to whip him—and for Jesse to run away—while he never whipped me and seldom spoke harshly to me, let me go with him everywhere, stand right by him while he poured the steps for the back porch, and ride with him when he peddled vegetables.

I made up my mind then. I would leave and I wasn't ever coming back. Talking to me like that, trying to turn my father against me . . . . She wouldn't ever see me anymore.

I went out to the store and asked my father for some money. The store was full of Sunday-school children buy- ing cold drinks and peanuts. I looked at them all dressed up, feeling that if I could get away I'd never see them again. He gave me a quarter and I left the yard, walking with a bunch that was laughing and talking and drinking their cold drinks. One by one they dropped off, but I kept walking. I was on my way to the bus line. I had never ridden the bus, but I knew where it turned around; that was about two miles away. Aunt Jo lived in town now, and so did my father's cousins, and if I could get to them, they would help me; perhaps I could stay with them. I could finish school in town and I wouldn't have to come to Wildwood anymore.

Soon I was near the highway and alone. Everybody else was at home or at a friend's house, where they had asked permission to stop. The highway was different. There were fewer houses, but I had traveled this way hundreds of times on my father's wagon. There was one house close to Wildwood, tall and two-storied, many-windowed, with flapping shutters, that I was afraid of. People said that there was a ghost in it and the ghost made noises late at night. Farther ahead were two homes, one on either side of the highway. Both of the families were rich, but they were not friends, for one family had "old" money and one family had "new" money. Hazel and her family lived with the Richardses, the family with the "old" money, on a "farm" that was really an estate. Hazel was very proud of their house. It had running water and was well kept up, for it was practically in the Richardses' yard. The Ransoms lived in a tree-shaded park, one that occupied the full time of several yard men, practically across the street from the Richardses, but Hazel liked to tell how the people her parents worked for would have nothing to do with them, for they had no "quality."

I walked on past the long hedge that separated the Ransoms' park from the highway, wondering how it must feel to live in a big house in a grove of trees, far away from the highway, never having to do anything, with a swarm of servants doing everything. Then I looked at the four-tiered white fence that surrounded the Richardses' "farm"; it took a long time to drive past it, and I knew that by the time I walked past it, I would be near the bus line.

Once when I was visiting Hazel, she proudly showed me the farm. There was a whole garage of nothing but old cars, all kinds, that used to belong to the family. Then she showed me the swimming pool and the barn where the cows were milked and the tennis courts. She was quite proud of the place; to her it was her "home."

Near the place where the Richardses' fence stopped, but across the highway, were little houses where other white people lived, those who didn't have the money that the Richardses had. Sometimes they sat on the porch and I wondered what they thought when they looked at all the Richardses had and compared it with what they had. From then on to the bus line, there were little houses, boxlike, with little lawns and hedges; the large estate and the farm were past.

When I got to the bus stop, there was no bus. I walked on, not really minding it, for the highway had become a street and now there was a sidewalk and I liked walking; so I continued, mile after mile, passing service stations, little box houses. I met a bus going to the end of the line when I was far down the street, and still I walked—past more service stations and hot-dog stands and small businesses and more houses. I felt so good that I thought that I would walk all the way in to town, thus saving my quarter.

Near the creek at the foot of Mangum Street hill a car passed me. At first I didn't notice it, but when someone yelled I looked up.

There were three or four white boys in the car. I

wondered what they had said, but I didn't really pay attention, for I was getting closer and closer to town and I was
preoccupied with wondering how I was going to make out.
Was someone going to invite me to stay? Would my
mother let me stay? Would a new life start for me? I hoped
so. I knew that my father would come and get me, and
maybe then I could tell him how Nonnie hurt me by talking
so mean to me all the time and he would make her stop.
But then he was sick all the time and dependent on her,
and besides, who would feed me, clothe me, give me
money to go to school? There was nobody who could but
Aunt Jo, and Nonnie wouldn't, I was sure, let me stay with
her. I walked along on a bright Sunday morning—it was
near noon by then—hoping that things would work out all
right.

Then a black car passed me again and someone threw ice
on me. I was scared, for the same car had circled around
and come back up on me from behind. White
people—they were the evil, the danger, that existed in the
world. You avoided them like snakes. I didn't know what
to do. Would they harass me from then on, constantly
circling and coming up from behind? I looked back and
saw the bus coming. It had gone to the end of the line and
waited and now was making a return trip; it was Sunday
and the buses weren't running frequently. So, never having
been on a bus, I stood at the foot of the hill where there
was a sign that said BUS, and when it came I got on. A
brief conversation with the driver got me three tokens.

I was surprised to see Nancy on the bus; she taught the
little children in Sunday school. She was surprised to see
me, too. I told her that I was going to town to see my folks.
She soon discovered that I knew nothing about changing
buses and getting a transfer, and told me how and where to

change. I went to the front and got the little pink transfer and got off at Walgreen's at Main Street.

I got to West Durham all right. I was proud of myself for finding the way, the first time on my own. I went to see Aunt Jo, but I felt so sad, for she was living in a small dark room in a house with two unmarried sisters. She didn't like it; I had heard her tell my mother that once. She asked me about everybody and I said they were all right, but I knew that she knew that something was wrong, because I had come alone. I wanted to tell her so much and I started to several times—that I wanted to come to town to live, maybe even stay with her; but I felt so bad that I would be letting her down, for she held me up as a model to her nieces and nephews, and if they knew I was running away from home it would make her look bad for having so much faith in me. I couldn't make the words come out. So we sat and talked, awkwardly, for we hadn't been alone in a long time. She spoke again of education. I must get an education.

I didn't know it then, but she was already dying of cancer. Marva, my older cousin, who lived across the street from Aunt Jo, was surprised to see me, and her daughter Jerline barely spoke—though she had been to visit us in the country—and an older male cousin took the extra token that I had put in a dish on the coffee table. I saw him take it, but he was grown and I was scared to say "Don't."

In the late afternoon I started back home. I rode the bus downtown all right, but at Five Points I didn't know how to change buses and was too scared to ask; so I started walking right on Main Street, in the heart of Durham. I walked the eight miles home.

Near the bus line Jesse met me; he was on his way to town. "Mama's gonna whip you!" He laughed in that

special way he had when something bad was going to happen to somebody. I said nothing, but walked on. It was
soon deep night. Wildwood was dark and quiet when I got
back, with a light here and there. I passed no one.

Nonnie was angry and I was defiant. She got her switches to whip me, but I started yelling that I was going to leave
again and I wasn't coming back. She did a lot of fussing,
but she hit me only a time or two. I knew that I had won,
for I never got another whipping. I had learned the value
of protest. And I, too, put my soul on ice. I had to, if I was
to survive.

THE SEVEN STOREY MOUNTAIN
by Thomas Merton

Thomas Merton, Trappist monk, poet, writer, contemplative, a man of depth and breadth, was born in France near the Spanish border during World War I. His father, an impecunious but talented artist, was a New Zealander and his mother an American. His father had hoped to settle in France and "raise a family, and paint, and live on practically nothing, because we had practically nothing to live on."

The young Merton felt that he had "inherited from my father his way of looking at things and some of his integrity and from my mother some of her dissatisfaction with the mess the world is in, and some of her versatility. From both I got capacities for work and vision and enjoyment and expression . . . "

He was educated at Cambridge and at Columbia. Merton, while at the latter, converted to Catholicism. Not long after graduation he joined the Trappist monastery at Gethsemane, Kentucky. His influence reached beyond American Catholics. Through his voluminous writings he became a celebrated monk. He died away from the monastery, in Thailand, of an electrical accident.

IN the three months, the summer of 1931, I suddenly matured like a weed.

I cannot tell which is the more humiliating: the memory of the half-baked adolescent I was in June or the glib and hard-boiled specimen I was in October when I came back to Oakham full of a thorough and deep-rooted sophistication of which I was both conscious and proud.

The beginning was like this: Pop wrote to me to come to America. I got a brand-new suit made. I said to myself, "On the boat I am going to meet a beautiful girl, and I am going to fall in love."

So I got on the boat. The first day I sat in a deck chair and read the correspondence of Goethe and Schiller which had been imposed on me as a duty, in preparation for the scholarship examinations at the university. What is worse, I not only tolerated this imposition but actually convinced myself that it was interesting.

The second day I had more or less found out who was on the boat. The third day I was no longer interested in Goethe and Schiller. The fourth day I was up to my neck in the trouble that I was looking for.

It was a ten-day boat.

I would rather spend two years in a hospital than go through that anguish again! That devouring, emotional, passionate love of adolescence that sinks its claws into you and consumes you day and night and eats into the vitals of your soul! All the self-tortures of doubt and anxiety and imagination and hope and despair that you go through when you are a child trying to break out of your shell, only to find yourself in the middle of a legion of full-armed emotions against which you have no defense! It is like being flayed alive. No one can go through it twice. This kind of a love affair can really happen only once in a man's life. After that he is calloused. He is no longer capable of so many torments. He can suffer, but not from so many matters of no account. After one such crisis he has experience and the possibility of a second time no longer exists, because the secret of the anguish was his own utter guilelessness. He is no longer capable of such complete and absurd surprises. No matter how simple a man may be, the obvious cannot go on astonishing him forever.

I was introduced to this particular girl by a Catholic priest who came from Cleveland and played shuffleboard in his shirt sleeves without a Roman collar on. He knew everybody on the boat in the first day, and as for me, two days had gone by before I even realized that she was on board. She was travelling with a couple of aunts and the three of them did not mix in with the other passengers very much. They kept to themselves in their three deck chairs and had nothing to do with the gentlemen in tweed caps and glasses who went breezing around and around the promenade deck.

When I first met her I got the impression she was no older than I was. As a matter of fact she was about twice my age: but you could be twice sixteen without being old, as I now realize, sixteen years after the event. She was small and delicate and looked as if she were made out of porcelain. But she had big wide-open California eyes and was not afraid to talk in a voice that was at once ingenuous and independent and had some suggestion of weariness about it as if she habitually stayed up too late at night.

To my dazzled eyes she immediately became the heroine of every novel and I all but flung myself face down on the deck at her feet. She could have put a collar on my neck and led me around from that time forth on the end of a chain. Instead of that I spent my days telling her and her aunts all about my ideals and my ambitions and she in her turn attempted to teach me how to play bridge. And that is the surest proof of her conquest, for I never allowed anyone else to try such a thing as that on me, never! But even she could not succeed in such an enterprise.

We talked. The insatiable wound inside me bled and grew, and I was doing everything I could to make it bleed more. Her perfume and the peculiar smell of the denicotinized cigarettes she smoked followed me everywhere and tortured me in my cabin.

She told me how once she was in a famous night club in a famous city when a famous person, a prince of the royal blood, had stared very intently at her for a long time and had finally got up and started to lurch in the direction of her table when his friends had made him sit down and behave himself.

I could see that all the counts and dukes who liked to marry people like Constance Bennett would want also to marry her. But the counts and dukes were not here on board this glorifed cargo boat that was carrying us all peacefuly across the mild dark waves of the North Atlantic. The thing that crushed me was that I had never learned to dance.

We made Natucket Light on Sunday afternoon and had to anchor in quarantine that night. So the ship rode in the Narrows on the silent waters, and the lights of Brooklyn glittered in the harbor like jewels. The boat was astir with music and with a warm glowing life that pulsated within the dark hull and poured out into the July night through every porthole. There were parties in all the cabins. Everywhere you went, especially on deck where it was quiet, you were placed in the middle of movie scenery—the setting for the last reel of the picture.

I made a declaration of my undying love. I would not, could not, ever love anyone else but her. It was impossible, unthinkable. If she went to the ends of the earth, destiny would bring us together again. The stars in their courses from the beginning of the world had plotted this meeting which was the central fact in the whole history of the universe. Love like this was immortal. It conquered time and outlasted the futility of human history. And so forth.

She talked to me, in her turn, gently and sweetly. What it sounded like was: "You do not know what you are saying. This can never be. We shall never meet again." What it meant was: "You are a nice kid. But for heaven's sake grow up before someone makes a fool of you." I went to my cabin and sobbed over my diary for a while and then, against all laws of romance, went peacefully to sleep.

However, I could not sleep for long. At five o'clock I was up again, and walking restlessly around the deck. It was hot. A grey mist lay on the Narrows. But when it became light, other anchored ships began to appear as shapes in the mist. One of them was a Red Star liner on which, as I learned from the papers when I got on shore, a passenger was at that precise moment engaged in hanging himself.

At the last minute before landing I took a snapshot of her which, to my intense sorrow, came out blurred. I was so avid for a picture of her that I got too close with the camera and it was out of focus. It was a piece of poetic justice that filled me with woe for months.

Of course the whole family was there on the dock. But the change was devastating. With my heart ready to explode with immature emotions I suddenly found myself surrounded by all the cheerful and peaceful and comfortable solicitudes of home. Everybody wanted to talk. Their voices were full of questions and information. They took me for a drive on Long Island and showed me where Mrs. Hearst lived and everything. But I only hung my head out of the window of the car and watched the green trees go swirling by, and wished that I were dead.

I would not tell anybody what was the matter with me, and this reticence was the beginning of a kind of estrangement between us. From that time on no one could be sure what I was doing or thinking. I would go to New York and I would not come home for meals and I would not tell anyone where I had been.

Most of the time I had not been anywhere special; I would go to the movies, and then wander around the streets and look at the crowds of people and eat hot dogs and drink orange juice at Nedicks. Once with great excitement I got inside a speak-easy. And when I found out that the place was raided a few days later I grew so much in my own estimation that I began to act as if I had shot my way out of the wildest joints in town.

Bonnemaman was the one who suffered most from my reticence. For years she had been sitting at home wondering what Pop was doing in the city all day, and now that I was developing the same wandering habits it was quite natural for her to imagine strange things about me too.

But the only wickedness I was up to was that I roamed around the city smoking cigarettes and hugging my own sweet sense of independence.

I found out that Grossett and Dunlap published more than the Rover Boys. They brought out reprints of writers like Hemingway and Aldous Huxley and D. H. Lawrence and I devoured them all, on the cool sleeping porch of the house at Douglaston, while the moths of the summer darkness came batting and throbbing against the screens attracted by my light that burned until all hours.

Most of the time I was running into my uncle's room to borrow his dictionary, and when he found out what words I was looking up he arched his brows and said: "What are you reading, anyway?"

At the end of the summer I started back for England on the same boat on which I had come. This time the passenger list included some girls from Bryn Mawr and some from Vassar and some from somewhere else, all of whom were going to a finishing school in France. It seems as if all the rest of the people on board were detectives. Some of them were professional detectives. Others were amateurs; all of them made me and the Bryn Mawr girls the object of their untiring investigations. But in any case the ship was divided into these two groups: on the one hand the young people, on the other the elders. We sat in the smoking room all the rainy days playing Duke Ellington records on the portable vic that belonged to one of the girls. When we got tired of that we wandered all over the ship looking for funny things to do. The hold was full of cattle, and there was also a pack of fox-hounds down there. We used to go down and play with the dogs. At Le Havre, when the cattle were unloaded, some of the cows broke loose and ran all over the dock in a frenzy. One night three of us got up in the crow's nest of the foremast, where we certainly did not belong. Another time we had a party with the radio operators and I got into a big argument about Communism.

That was another thing that had happened that summer: I had begun to get the idea that I was a Communist, although I wasn't quite sure what Communism was. There are a lot of people like that. They do no little harm by virtue of their sheer, stupid inertia, lost in between all camps, in the no-man's-land of their own confusion. They are fair game for anybody. They can be turned into fascists just as quickly as they can be pulled into line with those who are really Reds.

The other group was made up of the middle-aged people. At their core were the red-faced hard-boiled cops who spent their time drinking and gambling and fighting among themselves and spreading scandal all over the boat about the young ones who were so disreputable and wild.

The truth is that we did have quite a big bar bill, the Bryn Mawr girls and myself, but we were never drunk, because we drank slowly and spent the whole time stuffing ourselves with sardines on toast and all the other dainties which are the stock in trade of English liners.

In any case, I set foot once more on the soil of England dressed up in a gangster suit which Pop had bought me at Wallach's, complete with padded shoulders. And I had a new, pale grey hat over my eye and walked into England pleased with the consciousness that I had easily acquired a very lurid reputation for myself with scarcely any trouble at all.

The separation of the two generations on board the ship had pleased me. It had flattered me right down to the soles of my feet. It was just what I wanted. It completed my self-confidence, guaranteed my self-assertion. Anyone older than myself symbolized authority. And the vulgarity of the detectives and the stupidity of the other middle-aged people who had believed all their stories about us fed me with a pleasantly justifiable sense of contempt for their whole generation. Therefore I concluded that I was now free of all authority, and that nobody could give me any advice that I had to listen to. Because advice was only the cloak of hypocrisy or weakness or vulgarity or fear. Authority was constituted by the old and weak, and had its roots in their envy for the joys and pleasures of the young and strong . . . .

Finally, when I arrived at Oakham several days after the beginning of the term I was convinced that I was the only one in the whole place who knew anything about life, from the Headmaster on down.

A CHILD OF THE CENTURY
by Ben Hecht

Ben Hecht's stay at the University of Wisconsin has to have been among the shortest in the history of the University. His exit hurled him unwittingly into the newspaper world. Reluctant to face his mother, he ran away to Chicago. There, waiting in line to buy a ticket to the Majestic Vaudville Theatre, he met a distant uncle. Uncle Moyses, told by his nephew he was job-hunting (a lie), introduced him as a writer (a greater lie) to his friend John C. Eastman, Publisher of the Chicago Daily Journal. *Eastman ordered sixteen-year-old Ben to write a poem about a bull. This he did and was hired as a journalist.*

Upon being introduced to the city editor he was asked if he had any experience on a newspaper:

Ben Hecht: Only today.

Editor: What did you do today?

Ben Hecht: I wrote a poem for Mr. Eastman about a bull.

Editor (in a mutter): As a rule we prefer prose in our columns.

MY School days ended when I was sixteen, although other plans had been made for me. Who made these plans I do not remember, except that neither I nor my parents could have been responsible; neighbors, possibly, and some acquiescent bounderism on my part no doubt.

I enrolled in the summer of 1910 in the University of Wisconsin. I spent my first two days lurking about in the fraternity house to which I had been pledged, fascinated by the high stiff collars my brothers-to-be insisted on wearing on the premises, despite the heat and the fact that there were no womenfolk to badger them. I was unusually silent, for these high stiff collars undermined my ego. On the second evening one of the students informed me he was off to keep a date with a chorus girl with whom he was going to spend the entire night, as he put it, pasted together. This phrase is all I remember of my college days, which ended abruptly the next afternoon.

On the third morning I went to an office and selected a course of education with the amiable tag "Arts and Sciences." At the lunch table, one of the high collars, who also wore a gold lion's head stickpin in his tie, asked me if I had chosen my branch of learning. Thus openly invited to discourse by one of the flossiest of my hosts, I answered with a gush of confidence. I said that I had, but that I was greatly worried because, as far as I could make out, the university had nothing to teach me. I had already read nearly all the books listed in the Arts and Sciences prospectus.

After lunch my sponsor in the club, Jack Davies, with whom I had played football in high school, led me ominously to his room. He explained I would have to apologize to the house at the dinner table for having insulted the university. I agreed to do this.

At six o'clock I started downstairs to speak my piece of apology to the stiff collars. But I was unable to enter the room in which they sat waiting as stonily, I was certain, as a gallery of Cauchons prepared for the entrance of the heretic maid, Joan. Instead, I made for the front door and bolted into the summer evening. I trotted through the streets of Madison, full of misery. An hour later I was on a train going to Chicago—and out of universities forever.

FIFTH CHINESE DAUGHTER
by Jade Snow Wong

So mindful of Chinese propriety was Jade Snow Wong that she would not write her autobiography, although in English, using the customary "I." Instead she employed the third person. In written Chinese prose or poetry the word "I" almost never appears—it would be a betrayal of the expected submergence of the individual. But its eschewal did not stop with literature. When Jade Snow wrote her father she would write in words half the size of the regular ideographs "small daughter Jade Snow," in referring to herself. Her father writing to her would refer to himself in the third person.

Jade Snow grew up in San Francisco between the two World Wars. Her autobiography covers her first twenty-four years, years in which she was surrounded by the careful, restrained customs of her Chinese family but years, too, during which she gradually became aware of another culture.

Not until almost the end of her senior year in high school was she a part of a mixed crowd of friends without a chaperone. The occasion was a dance given by the Chinese Students Club at the girls' high school which she attended. Because at that time Jade Snow was living with an American family for whom she did housework she did not have to ask parental permission to attend the dance—a permission that probably would not have been forthcoming. Two highlights marked the evening of the dance for her: she learned how to dance and she met Joe who became a good friend and who strongly encouraged her to attend college.

Jade Snow's careful observance of Chinese custom did not keep her from deciding, independent of parental advice, to go to college. For a Chinese American girl of sixteen this was a daring decision to reach independently of her family.

She had hoped to go to the state university but did not receive the necessary scholarship. Her friend, Joe, would not let her give up the idea of college and persuaded her to register at a junior college.

SO, without much enthusiasm, Jade Snow decided upon junior college. Now it was necessary to inform Mama and Daddy. She chose an evening when the family was at dinner. All of them were in their customary places, and Daddy, typically, was in conversation with Older Brother about the factory:

"Blessing, when do you think Lot Number fifty-one twenty-six will be finished? I want to ask for a check from our jobber so that I can have enough cash for next week's payroll."

To which Older Brother replied, "As soon as Mama is through with the seams in Mrs. Lee's and Mrs. Choy's bundles, the women can finish the hems. Another day, probably."

Mama had not been consulted; therefore she made no comment. Silence descended as the Wongs continued their meal, observing the well-learned precept that talk was not permissible while eating.

Jade Snow considered whether to break the silence. Three times she thought over what she had to say, and still she found it worth saying. This also was according to family precept.

"Daddy," she said, "I have made up my mind to enter

junior college here in San Francisco. I will find a steady job to pay my expenses, and by working in the summers I'll try to save enough money to take me through my last two years at the university.''

Then she waited. Everyone went on eating. No one said a word. Apparently no one was interested enough to be curious. But at least no one objected. It was settled.

Junior college was at first disappointing in more ways than one. There was none of the glamour usually associated with college because the institution was so young that it had not yet acquired buildings of its own. Classes were held all over the city wherever accommodations were available. The first days were very confusing to Jade Snow, especially when she discovered that she must immediately decide upon a college major.

While waiting to register, she thumbed through the catalogue in search of a clue. English . . . mathematics . . . chemistry . . . . In the last semester of high school she had found chemistry particularly fascinating: so with a feeling of assurance she wrote that as her major on the necessary forms, and went to a sign-up table.

"I wish to take the lecture and laboratory classes for Chemistry 1A," she informed the gray-haired man who presided there.

He looked at her, a trifle impatiently she thought.

"Why?"

"Because I like it." To herself she sounded reasonable.

"But you are no longer in high school. Chemistry here is a difficult subject on a university level, planned for those who are majoring in medicine, engineering, or the serious sciences."

Jade Snow set her chin stubbornly. "I still want to take Chemistry 1A."

Sharply he questioned: "What courses in mathematics

have you had? What were your grades?''

Finally Jade Snow's annoyance rose to the surface. "Straight A's. But why must you ask? Do you think I would want to take a course I couldn't pass? Why don't you sign me up and let the instructor be the judge of my ability?"

"Very well," he replied stiffly. "I'll accept you in the class. And for your information, young lady, I am the instructor!"

With this inauspicious start, Jade Snow began her college career.

To take care of finances, she now needed to look for work. Through a friend she learned that a Mrs. Simpson needed someone to help with household work. "Can you cook?" was Mrs. Simpson's first question.

Jade Snow considered a moment before answering. Certainly she could cook Chinese food, and she remembered a common Chinese saying, "A Chinese can cook foreign food as well as, if not better than, the foreigners, but a foreigner cannot cook Chinese food fit for the Chinese." On this reasoning it seemed safe to say "Yes."

Of her college courses, Latin was the easiest. This was a surprise, for everyone had told her of its horrors. It was much more logical than French, almost mathematical in its orderliness and precision, and actually a snap after nine years of Chinese.

Chemistry, true to the instructor's promise, was difficult, although the classes were anything but dull. It turned out that he was a very nice person with a keen sense of humor and a gift for enlivening his lectures with stories of his own college days. There were only two girls in a class of more than fifty men—a tense blonde girl from Germany, who always ranked first; and Jade Snow, who usually took second place.

But if Latin was the easiest course and chemistry the most difficult, sociology was the most stimulating. Jade Snow had chosen it without thought, simply to meet a requirement; but that casual decision completely revolutionized her thinking, shattering her Wong-constructed conception of the order of things. This was the way it happened:

After several uneventful weeks during which the class explored the historical origins of the family and examined such terms as "norms," "mores," "folkways," there came a day when the instructor stood before them to discuss the relationship of parents and children. It was a day like many others, with the students listening in varying attitudes of interest or indifference. The instructor was speaking casually of ideas to be accepted as standard. Then suddenly upon Jade Snow's astounded ears there fell this statement:

"There was a period in our American history when parents had children for economic reasons, to put them to work as soon as possible, especially to have them help on the farm. But now we no longer regard children in this way. Today we recognize that children are individuals, and that parents can no longer demand their unquestioning obedience. Parents should do their best to understand their children, because young people also have their rights."

The instructor went on talking, but Jade Snow heard no more, for her mind was echoing and re-echoing this startling thought. "Parents can no longer demand unquestioning obedience from their children. They should do their best to understand. Children also have their rights." For the rest of the day, while she was doing her chores at the

Simpsons', while she was standing in the streetcar going home, she was busy translating the idea into terms of her own experience.

"My parents demand unquestioning obedience. Older Brother demands unquestioning obedience. By what right? I am an individual besides being a Chinese daughter. I have rights too."

Could it be that Daddy and Mama, although they were living in San Francisco in the year 1938, actually had not left the Chinese world of thirty years ago? Could it be that they were forgetting that Jade Snow would soon become a woman in a new America, not a woman in old China? In short, was it possible that Daddy and Mama could be wrong?

For days Jade Snow gave thought to little but her devastating discovery that her parents might be subject to error. As it was her habit always to act after reaching a conclusion, she wondered what to do about it. Should she tell Daddy and Mama that they needed to change their ways? One moment she thought she should, the next she thought not. At last she decided to overcome her fear in the interest of education and better understanding. She would at least try to open their minds to modern truths. If she succeeded, good! If not, she was prepared to suffer the consequences.

In this spirit of patient martyrdom she waited for an opportunity to speak.

It came, surprisingly, one Saturday. Ordinarily that was a busy day at the Simpsons', a time for entertaining, so that Jade Snow was not free until too late to go anywhere even had she had a place to go. But on this particular Saturday the Simpsons were away for the weekend, and by three in the afternoon Jade Snow was ready to leave the apartment with unplanned hours ahead of her. She didn't want to spend these rare hours of freedom in any usual way, and she didn't want to spend them alone.

"Shall I call Joe?" she wondered. She had never telephoned to a boy before and she debated whether it would be too forward. But she felt too happy and carefree to worry much, and she was confident that Joe would not misunderstand.

Even before reporting to Mama that she was home, she ran downstairs to the telephone booth and gave the operator Joe's number. His mother answered and then went to call him while Jade Snow waited in embarrassment.

"Joe." She was suddenly tongue-tied. "Joe, I'm already home."

That wasn't at all what she wanted to say. What did she want to say?

"Hello! Hello!" Joe boomed back. "What's the matter with you? Are you all right?"

"Oh, yes, I'm fine. Only, only . . . well, I'm through working for the day." That was really all she had to say, but now it sounded rather pointless.

"Isn't that wonderful? It must have been unexpected." That was what was nice and different about Joe. He always seemed to know without a lot of words. But because his teasing was never far behind his understanding he added quickly, "I suppose you're going to study and go to bed early."

Jade Snow was still not used to teasing and didn't know how to take it. With an effort she swallowed her shyness and disappointment. "I thought we might go for a walk . . . that is, if you have nothing else to do . . . if you would care to . . . if . . . "

Joe laughed. "I'll go you one better. Suppose I take you to a movie. I'll even get all dressed up for you, and you get dressed up too."

Jade Snow was delighted. Her first movie with Joe! What a wonderful day. In happy anticipation she put on her long silk stockings, lipstick, and the nearest thing to a suit she owned—a hand-me-down jacket and a brown skirt she had made herself. Then with a bright ribbon tying back her long black hair she was ready.

Daddy didn't miss a detail of the preparations as she dashed from room to room. He waited until she was finished before he demanded, "Jade Snow, where are you going?"

"I am going out into the street," she answered.

"Did you ask my permission to go out into the street?"

"No, Daddy."

"Do you have your mother's permission to go out into the street?"

"No, Daddy."

A sudden silence from the kitchen indicated that Mama was listening.

Daddy went on: "Where and when did you learn to be so daring as to leave this house without permission of your parents? You did not learn it under my roof."

It was all very familiar. Jade Snow waited, knowing that Daddy had not finished. In a moment he came to the point.

"And with whom are you going out into the street?"

It took all the courage Jade Snow could muster, remembering her new thinking, to say nothing. It was certain that if she told Daddy that she was going out with a boy whom he did not know, without a chaperone, he would be convinced that she would lose her maidenly purity before the evening was over.

"Very well," Daddy said sharply. "If you will not tell me, I forbid you to go! You are now too old to whip."

That was the moment.

Suppressing all anger, and in a manner that would have done credit to her sociology instructor addressing his freshman class, Jade Snow carefully turned on her mentally rehearsed speech.

"That is something you should think more about. Yes, I am too old to whip. I am too old to be treated as a child. I can now think for myself, and you and Mama should not demand unquestioning obedience from me. You should understand me. There was a time in America when parents raised children to make them work, but now the foreigners regard them as individuals with rights of their own. I have worked too, but now I am an individual besides being your fifth daughter."

It was almost certain that Daddy blinked, but after the briefest pause he gathered himself together.

"Where," he demanded, "did you learn such an unfilial theory?"

Mama had come quietly into the room and slipped into a chair to listen.

"From my teacher," Jade Snow answered triumphantly, "who you taught me is supreme after you, and whose judgment I am not to question."

Daddy was feeling pushed. Thoroughly aroused, he shouted:

"A little learning has gone to your head! How can you permit a foreigner's theory to put aside the practical experience of the Chinese, who for thousands of years have preserved a most superior family pattern? Confucius had already presented an organized philosophy of manners and conduct when the foreigners were unappreciatively persecuting Christ. Who brought you up? Who clothed you, fed you, sheltered you, nursed you? Do you think you were born aged sixteen? You owe honor to us before you satisfy your personal whims.''

Daddy thundered on, while Jade Snow kept silent.

''What would happen to the order of this household if each of you four children started to behave like individuals? Would we have one peaceful moment if your personal desires came before your duty? How could we maintain our self-respect if we, your parents, did not know where you were at night and with whom you were keeping company?''

With difficulty Jade Snow kept herself from being swayed by fear and the old familiar arguments. ''You can be bad in the daytime as well as at night,'' she said defensively. ''What could happen after eleven that couldn't happen before?''

Daddy was growing more excited. ''Do I have to justify my judgment to you? I do not want a daughter of mine to be known as one who walks the streets at night. Have you no thought for our reputations if not for your own? If you start going out with boys, no good man will want to ask you to be his wife. You just do not know as well as we do what is good for you.''

Mama fanned Daddy's wrath, ''Never having been a mother, you cannot know how much grief it is to bring up a daughter. Of course we will not permit you to run the risk of corrupting your purity before marriage.''

''Oh, Mama!'' Jade Snow retorted. ''This is America, not China. Don't you think I have any judgment? How can you think I would go out with just any man?''

''Men!'' Daddy roared. ''You don't know a thing about them. I tell you, you can't trust any of them.''

Now it was Jade Snow who felt pushed. She delivered the balance of her declaration of independence:

"Both of you should understand that I am growing up to be a woman in a society greatly different from the one you knew in China. You expect me to work my way through college—which would not have been possible in China. You expect me to exercise judgment in choosing my employers and my jobs and in spending my own money in the American world. Then why can't I choose my friends? Of course independence is not safe. But safety isn't the only consideration. You must give me the freedom to find some answers for myself."

Mama found her tongue first. "You think you are too good for us because you have a little foreign book knowledge."

"You will learn the error of your ways after it is too late," Daddy added darkly.

By this Jade Snow knew that her parents had conceded defeat. Hoping to soften the blow, she tried to explain: "If I am to earn my living, I must learn how to get along with many kinds of people, with foreigners as well as Chinese. I intend to start finding out about them now. You must have confidence that I shall remain true to the spirit of your teachings. I shall bring back to you the new knowledge of whatever I learn."

Daddy and Mama did not accept this offer graciously. "It is as useless for you to tell me such ideas as 'The wind blows across a deaf ear.' You have lost your sense of balance," Daddy told her bluntly. "You are shameless. You skin is yellow. Your features are forever Chinese. We are content with our proven ways. Do not try to force foreign ideas into my home. Go. You will one day tell us sorrowfully that you have been mistaken."

After that there was no further discussion of the matter. Jade Snow came and went without any questions being asked. In spite of her parents' dark predictions, her new freedom in the choice of companions did not result in a rush of undesirables. As a matter of fact, the boys she met at school were more concerned with copying her lecture notes than with anything else.

As for Joe, he remained someone to walk with and talk with. On the evening of Jade Snow's seventeenth birthday he took her up Telegraph Hill and gave her as a remembrance a sparkling grown-up bracelet with a card which read: "Here's to your making Phi Beta Kappa." And there under the stars he gently tilted her face and gave her her first kiss.

Standing straight and awkward in her full-skirted red cotton dress, Jade Snow was caught by surprise and without words. She felt that something should stir and crash within her, in the way books and the movies described, but nothing did. Could it be that she wasn't in love with Joe, in spite of liking and admiring him? After all, he was twenty-three and probably too old for her anyway.

Still she had been kissed at seventeen, which was cause for rejoicing. Laughing happily, they continued their walk.

But while the open rebellion gave Jade Snow a measure of freedom she had not had before, and an outer show of assurance, she was deeply troubled within. It had been simple to have Daddy and Mama tell her what was right and wrong; it was not simple to decide for herself. No matter how critical she was of them, she could not discard all they stood for and accept as a substitute the philosophy of the foreigners. It took very little thought to discover that the foreign philosophy also was subject to criticism, and that for her there had to be a middle way.

In particular, she could not reject the fatalism that was at the core of all Chinese thinking and behaviour, the belief that the broad pattern of an individual's life was ordained by fate although within that pattern he was capable of perfecting himself and accumulating a desirable store of good will. Should the individual not benefit by his good works, still the rewards would pass on to his children or his children's children. Epitomized by the proverbs: "I save your life, for your grandson might save mine," and "Heaven does not forget to follow the path a good man walks," this was a fundamental philosophy of Chinese life which Jade Snow found fully as acceptable as some of the so-called scientific reasoning expounded in the sociology class, where heredity and environment were assigned all the responsibility for personal success or failure.

There was good to be gained from both concepts if she could extract and retain her own personally applicable combination. She studied her neighbor in class, Stella Green, for clues. Stella had grown up reading Robert Louis Stevenson, learning to swim and play tennis, developing a taste for roast beef, mashed potatoes, sweets, aspirin tablets, and soda pop, and she looked upon her mother and father as friends. But it was very unlikely that she knew where her great-grandfather was born, or whether or not she was related to another strange Green she might chance to meet. Jade Snow had grown up reading Confucius, learning to embroider and cook rice, developing a taste for steamed fish and bean sprouts, tea, and herbs, and she thought of her parents as people to be obeyed. She not only knew where her ancestors were born but where they were buried, and how many chickens and roast pigs should be brought annually to their graves to feast their spirits. She knew all of the branches of the

Wong family, the relation of each to the other, and understood why Daddy must help support the distant cousins in China who bore the sole responsibility of carrying on the family heritage by periodic visits to the burial grounds in Fragrant Mountains. She knew that one could purchase in a Chinese stationery store the printed record of her family tree relating their Wong line and other Wong lines back to the original Wong ancestors. In such a scheme the individual counted for little weighed against the family, and after sixteen years it was not easy to sever roots.

There were, alas, no books or advisers to guide Jade Snow in her search for balance between the pull from two cultures. If she chose neither to reject nor accept *in toto*, she must sift both and make her decisions alone. It would not be an easy search. But pride and determination, which Daddy had given her, prevented any thought of turning back.

By the end of her first year of junior college, she had been so impressed by her sociology course that she changed her major to the social studies. Four years of college no longer seemed interminable . . . .

Hand in hand with a growing awareness of herself and her personal world, there was developing in her an awareness of and a feeling for the larger world beyond the familiar pattern. At eighteen, when Jade Snow compared herself with a diary record of herself at sixteen, she could see many points of difference. She was now an extremely serious young person, with a whole set of worries which she donned with her clothes each morning. The two years had made her a littler wiser in the ways of the world, a little more realistic, less of a dreamer, and she hoped more of a personality . . . .

On this eighteenth birthday, instead of the birthday cake which Americans considered appropriate, Daddy brought home a fresh-killed chicken which Mama cooked their favorite way by plunging it into a covered pot of boiling water, moving it off the flame and letting it stand for one hour, turning it once. Brushed with oil and sprinkled with shredded fresh green onions, it retained its sweet flavor with all its juices, for it was barely cooked and never dry. It was the Wongs usual birthday dish. Naturally, the birthday of a daughter did not call for the honor due a parent. There was a birthday tea ritual calling for elaborate preparation when Mama's and Daddy's anniversaries came around. Still, to be a girl and eighteen was exciting.

The rest of the year rushed to an end. The years at junior college had been rewarding. Now several happy surprises climaxed them. First there was the satisfaction of election to membership in Alpha Gamma Sigma, an honorary state scholastic organization. On the advice of her English instructor, this precipitated an exchange of letters with an executive of the society concerning a possible scholarship to the university.

In the meantime, overtiredness and overwork brought on recurring back pains which confined Jade Snow to bed for several days. Against her will because she could not afford it, she had been driven to see a doctor, who told her to put a board under her mattress for back support, and gave her two prescriptions to be filled for relief of pain. But there was no money for medicine. She asked Daddy and Mama, who said that they could not afford to pay for it either. So Jade Snow went miserably to bed to stay until the pain should end of its own accord.

She had been there two days when Older Brother entered casually and tossed a letter on her bed. It was from the scholarship chairman of Alpha Gamma Sigma, enclosing a check for fifty dollars. It was an award to her as the most outstanding woman student of the junior colleges in California. Jade Snow's emotions were mixed. What she had wanted and needed was a full scholarship. On the other hand, recognition was sweet—a proof that God had not forgotten her.

On the heels of this letter came another from her faculty adviser, inviting her as one of the ten top-ranking students to compete for position as commencement speaker. "If you care to try out," it concluded, "appear at Room 312 on April 11 at ten o'clock."

Should she or should she not? She had never made a speech in public, and the thought was panic. But had she a right to refuse? Might not this be an opportunity to answer effectively all the "Richards" of the world who screamed "Chinky, Chinky, Chinaman" at her and other Chinese? Might it not be further evidence to offer her family that her decision had not been wrong?

It seemed obvious that the right thing to do was to try, and equally obvious that she should talk about what was most familiar to her: the values which she as an American-Chinese had found in two years of junior college.

At the try-out, in a dry voice, she coaxed out her prepared thesis and fled, not knowing whether she had been good or bad, and not caring. She was glad just to be done. A few days later came formal notification that she would be the salutatorian at graduation. She was terrified as she envisioned the stage at the elegant San Francisco War Memorial Opera House, with its tremendous sparkling chandelier and overpowering tiers of seats. Now she wished that she could escape.

The reality was as frightening as the anticipation when on June 7, 1940, she stood before the graduation audience, listening to her own voice coming over the loudspeaker.

All her family were there among the neat rows of faces before her. What did they think, hearing her say, "The Junior College has developed our initiative, fair play, and self-expression, and has given us tools for thinking and analyzing. But it seems to me that the most effective application that America-Chinese can make of their education would be in China, which needs all the Chinese talent she can muster."

Thus Jade Snow—shaped by her father's and mother's unceasing loyalty toward their mother country, impressed with China's needs by speakers who visited Chinatown, revolutionized by American ideas, fired with enthusiasm for social service—thought that she had quite independently arrived at the perfect solution for the future of all thinking and conscientious young Chinese, including herself. Did her audience agree with her conclusion?

At last it was over, the speeches and applause, the weeping and excited exchange of congratulations. According to plan, Jade Snow met her family on the steps of the Opera House, where they were joined shortly by her faculty adviser and her English professor. Conversation proceeded haltingly, as Daddy and Mama spoke only Chinese.

Mama took the initiative: "Thank your teachers for me for all the kind assistance they have given you. Ask them to excuse my not being able to speak English."

"Yes, indeed," Daddy added. "A fine teacher is very rare."

When Jade Snow had duly translated the remarks, she took advantage of a pause to inquire casually, "How was my speech?"

Mama was noncommittal. "I can't understand English."

"You talked too fast at first," was Older Brother's opinion.

Daddy was more encouraging: "It could be considered

passable. For your first speech, that was about it."

The subject was closed. Daddy had spoken. But there was a surprise in store.

"Will you ask your teachers to join us for late supper at a Chinese restaurant?" Daddy suggested.

"What restaurant?" Jade Snow wanted to know, bewildered.

"Tao-Tao on Jackson Street. I have made reservations and ordered food."

Hardly able to credit her senses, Jade Snow trailed after the party. At first she was apprehensive, feeling it her responsibility to make the guests comfortable and at ease in the strange surroundings. But her fears were unfounded. The guests genuinely enjoyed the novel experience of breaking bread with the Wongs. It was a thoroughly happy and relaxed time for everyone as they sat feasting on delicious stuffed-melon soup, Peking duck, steamed thousand-layer buns, and tasty crisp greens.

The whole day had been remarkable, but most remarkable of all was the fact that for the first time since her break with her parents, Mama and Daddy had granted her a measure of recognition and acceptance. For the first time they had met on common ground with her American associates. It was a sign that they were at last tolerant of her effort to search for her own pattern of life.

ALL QUIET ON THE WESTERN FRONT
by Erich Maria Remarque

In this deservedly renowned anti-war novel, a young Ger-
man, Paul Bäumer, tells the harrowing and moving story
of eight soldiers in the First World War. They find that
"renunciation of personality" was demanded while being
"trained for heroism as though they were circus ponies."
Their real education came, however, under fire.

Many battles later Bäumer, in the hospital recuperating
from wounds, muses: "I am young, I am twenty years old;
yet I know nothing of life but despair, death, fear . . . I
see how people are set against one another . . . . What
do they expect of us if a time ever comes when the war is
over? Through the years our business has been killing; it
was our first calling in life. Our knowledge of life is limited
to death. What will happen afterwards? And what shall
come out of us?"

Paul Bäumer need not have worried how he himself
would disentangle life and death. He dies shortly before
the war's end on a day so quiet and still that the army
report noted only a single sentence, "All quiet on the
western front."

The novel's author, Erich Maria Remarque, like its nar-

rator, went from high school to the German trenches. Except when recuperating from wounds he served at the front until the Armistice.

In the difficult post-war years Remarque held several different jobs but spent much time on his first novel, All Quiet on the Western Front, *published in Germany in 1928. There it quickly sold over a million copies. The book won him an international reputation, and by now is in more than twenty-five languages.*

When Hitler came to power Remarque left Germany for Switzerland. In 1939 he came to America where in 1947 he became a citizen. Eventually he returned to Switzerland living there until his death in 1970.

WE are at rest five miles behind the front. Yesterday we were relieved, and now our bellies are full of beef and haricot beans. We are satisfied and at peace. Each man has another mess-tin full for the evening; and, what is more, there is a double ration of sausage and bread. That puts a man in fine trim. We have not had such luck as this for a long time. The cook with his carroty head is begging us to eat; he beckons with his ladle to everyone that passes, and spoons him out a great dollop. He does not see how he can empty his stew-pot in time for coffee. Tjaden and Müller have produced two wash-basins and had them filled up to the brim for reserve. In Tjaden this is voracity, in Müller it is foresight. Where Tjaden puts it all is a mystery, for he is and always will be as thin as a rake.

What's more important still is the issue of a double ration of smokes. Ten cigars, twenty cigarettes, and two quids of chew per man; now that is decent. I have exchanged my chewing tobacco with Katczinsky for his cigarettes, which means I have forty altogether. That's enough for a day.

It is true we have no right to this windfall. The Prussian is not so generous. We have only a miscalculation to thank for it.

Fourteen days ago we had to go up and relieve the front line. It was fairly quiet on our sector, so the quartermaster who remained in the rear had requisitioned the usual quantity of rations and provided for the full company of one hundred and fifty men. But on the last day an astonishing number of English field-guns opened up on us with high-explosive, drumming ceaselessly on our position, so that we suffered heavily and came back only eighty strong.

Last night we moved back and settled down to get a good sleep for once: Katczinsky is right when he says it would not be such a bad war if only one could get a little more sleep. In the line we have had next to none, and fourteen days is a long time at one stretch.

It was noon before the first of us crawled out of our quarters. Half an hour later every man had his mess-tin and we gathered at the cook-house, which smelt greasy and nourishing. At the head of the queue of course were the hungriest—little Albert Kropp, the clearest thinker among us and therefore the first to be lance-corporal; Müller, who still carries his school textbooks with him, dreams of examinations, and during a bombardment mutters propositions in physics; Leer, who wears a full beard and has a preference for the girls from officers' brothels. He swears that they are obliged by an army order to wear silk chemises and to bathe before entertaining guests of the rank of major and upwards. And as the fourth, myself, Paul Bäumer. All four are nineteen years of age, and all four joined up from the same class as volunteers for the war.

Close behind us were our friends: Tjaden, a skinny locksmith of our own age, the biggest eater of the company. He sits down to eat as thin as a grasshopper and gets up as big as a bug in the family way; Haie Westhus, of the same age, a peat-digger, who can easily hold a ration-loaf in his hand and say: Guess what I've got in my fist; then Detering, a peasant, who thinks of nothing but his farm-yard and his wife; and finally Stanislaus Katczinsky, the leader of our group, shrewd, cunning, and hard-bitten, forty years of age, with a face of the soil, blue eyes, bent shoulders, and a remarkable nose for dirty weather, good food, and soft jobs.

Our gang formed the head of the queue before the cookhouse. We were growing impatient, for the cook paid no attention to us.

Finally, Katczinsky called out to him: "Say, Heinrich, open up the soup-kitchen. Anyone can see the beans are done."

He shook his head sleepily: "You must all be there first." Tjaden grinned: "We are all here."

The sergeant-cook still took no notice. "That may do for you," he said. "But where are the others?"

"They won't be fed by you to-day. They're either in the dressing-station or pushing up daisies."

The cook was quite disconcerted as the facts dawned on him. He was staggered. "And I have cooked for one hundred and fifty men—"

Kropp poked him in the ribs: "Then for once we'll have enough. Come on, begin!"

Suddenly a vision came over Tjaden. His sharp, mousey features began to shine, his eyes grew small with cunning, his jaws twitched, and he whispered hoarsely: "Man! then you've got bread for one hundred and fifty men too, eh?"

The sergeant-cook nodded, absent-minded and bewildered.

"Tjaden seized him by the tunic. "And sausage?"

Ginger nodded again.

Tjaden's chaps quivered. "Tobacco too?"

"Yes, everything."

Tjaden beamed: "What a bean-feast! That's all for us! Each man gets—wait a bit—yes, practically two issues."

Then Ginger stirred himself and said: "That won't do."

Then we got excited and began to crowd around.

"Why won't that do, you old carrot?" demanded Katczinsky.

"Eighty men can't have what is meant for a hundred and fifty."

"We'll soon show you," growled Müller.

"I don't care about the stew, but I can only issue rations for eighty men," persisted Ginger.

Katczinsky got angry. "You might be generous for once. you haven't drawn food for eighty men. You've drawn it for the Second Company. Good. Let's have it then. We are the Second Company."

We began to jostle the fellow. No one felt kindly toward him, for it was his fault that the food twice came up to us in the line too late and cold. Under shell-fire he wouldn't bring his kitchen up near enough, so that our soup-carriers had to go much farther than those of the other companies. Now Bulcke of the First Company is a much better fellow. He is as fat as a hamster in winter, but he trundles his pots when it comes to that right up to the very front line.

We were in just the right mood, and there would certainly have been a dust-up if our company commander had not appeared. He informed himself of the dispute, and only remarked: "Yes, we did have heavy losses yesterday."

He looked in the dixie. "The beans look good."

Ginger nodded. "Cooked with meat and fat."

The lieutenant looked at us. He knew what we were thinking. And he knew many other things too, because he came to the company as a non-com. and was promoted from the ranks. He lifted the lid from the dixie again and sniffed. Then passing on he said: "Serve out the whole issue. We can do with it. And bring me a plate full too."

Ginger looked sheepish as Tjaden danced around him.

"It doesn't cost you anything! One would think the quartermaster's store belonged to him! And now get on with it, you old blubber-sticker, and don't you miscount either."

"You be hanged!" spat out Ginger. When things get beyond him he throws up the sponge altogether; he just goes to pieces. And as if to show that all things were now the same to him, of his own free will he shared out half a pound of synthetic honey equally among us.

* * *

To-day is wonderfully good. The mail has come, and almost every man has a couple of letters and papers. We stroll over to the meadow behind the billets. Kropp has the round lid of a margarine tub under his arm.

On the right side of the meadow a large common latrine has been built, a well-planned and durable construction. But that is for recruits who as yet have not learned how to make the most of whatever comes their way. We look for something better. Scattered about everywhere there are separate, individual boxes for the same purpose. They are square, neat boxes with wooden sides all round, and have unimpeachably satisfactory seats. On the sides are hand-grips enabling one to shift them about.

We move three together in a ring and sit down comfortably. For two hours we have been here without getting up.

I well remember how embarrassed we were as recruits in barracks when we had to use the general latrine. There were no doors and twenty men sat side by side as in a railway carriage, so that they could be reviewed all at one glance, for soldiers must always be under supervision.

Since then we have learned better than to be shy about such trifling immodesties. In time things far worse than that came easy to us.

Here in the open air though, the business is entirely a pleasure. I no longer understand why we should always have shied at it before. It is, in fact, just as natural as eating and drinking. We did not properly appreciate these boxes when we first enlisted; they were new to us and did not fill such an important role—but now they have long been a matter of course.

The soldier is on friendlier terms than other men with his stomach and intestines. Three-quarters of his vocabulary is derived from these regions, and they give an intimate flavour to expressions of his greatest joy as well as of his deepest indignation. It is impossible to express oneself in any other way so clearly and pithily. Our families and our teachers will be shocked when we go home, but here it is the universal language.

Enforced publicity has in our eyes restored the character of complete innocence to all these things. More than that, they are so much a matter of course that their comfortable performance is fully as much enjoyed as the playing of a safe top running flush. Not for nothing was the word "latrine-rumour" invented; these places are the regimental gossip-shops and common-rooms.

We feel ourselves for the time being better off than in any palatial white-tiled "convenience." *There* it can only be hygienic; *here* it is beautiful.

These are wonderfully care-free hours. Over us is the blue sky. On the horizon float the bright yellow, sunlit observation-balloons, and the many little white clouds of the anti-aircraft shells. Often they rise in a sheaf as they follow after an airman. We hear the muffled rumble of the front only as very distant thunder, bumble-bees droning by quite drown it. Around us stretches the flowery meadow. The grasses sway their tall spears; the white butterflies flutter around and float on the soft warm wind of the late summer. We read letters and newspapers and smoke. We take off our caps and lay them down beside us. The wind plays with our hair; it plays with our words and thoughts. The three boxes stand in the midst of the glowing, red field-poppies.

We set the lid of the margarine tub on our knees and so have a good table for a game of skat. Kropp has the cards with him. After every throw-in the loser pays into the pool. One could sit like this for ever.

The notes of an accordion float across from the billets. Often we lay aside the cards and look about us. One of us will say: "Well, boys . . . . " Or "It was a near thing that time . . . . " And for a moment we fall silent. There is in each of us a feeling of constraint. We are all sensible of it; it needs no words to communicate it. It might easily have happened that we should not be sitting here on our boxes to-day; it came damn near to that. And so everything is new and brave, red poppies and good food, cigarettes and summer breeze.

Kropp asks: "Anyone seen Kemmerich lately?"

"He's up at St. Joseph's," I tell him.

Müller explains that he has a flesh wound in his thigh; a good blighty.

We decide to go and see him this afternoon.

Kropp pulls out a letter. "Kantorek sends you all his best wishes."

We laugh. Muller throws his cigarette away and says: "I wish he was here."

* * *

Kantorek had been our schoolmaster, an active little man in a grey tail-coat, with a face like a shrew-mouse. He was about the same size as Corporal Himmelstoss, the "Terror of Klosterberg." It is very queer that the unhappiness of the world is so often brought on by small men. They are so much more energetic and uncompromising than the big fellows. I have always taken good care to keep out of sections with small company commanders. They are mostly confounded little martinets.

During drill-time Kantorek gave us long lectures until the whole of our class went under his shepherding to the District Commandant and volunteered. I can see him now, as he used to glare at us through his spectacles and say in a moving voice: "Won't you join up, Comrades?"

These teachers always carry their feelings ready in their waistcoat pockets, and fetch them out at any hour of the day. But we didn't think of that then.

There was, indeed, one of us who hesitated and did not want to fall into line. That was Josef Behm, a plump, homely fellow. But he did allow himself to be persuaded, otherwise he would have been ostracized. And perhaps more of us thought as he did, but no one could very well stand out, because at that time even one's parents were ready with the word "coward"; no one had the vaguest idea what we were in for. The wisest were just the poor and simple people. They knew the war to be a misfortune, whereas people who were better off were beside themselves with joy, though they should have been much better able to judge what the consequences would be.

Katczinsky said that was a result of their upbringing. It made them stupid. And what Kat said, he had thought about.

Strange to say, Behm was one of the first to fall. He got hit in the eye during an attack, and we left him lying for dead. We couldn't bring him with us, because we had to come back helter-skelter. In the afternoon suddenly we heard him call, and saw him outside creeping towards us. He had only been knocked unconscious. Because he could not see, and was mad with pain, he failed to keep under cover, and so was shot down before anyone could go and fetch him in.

Naturally we couldn't blame Kantorek for this. Where would the world be if one brought every man to book? There were thousands of Kantoreks, all of whom were convinced that there was only one way of doing well, and that way theirs.

And that is just why they let us down so badly.

For us lads of eighteen they ought to have been mediators and guides to the world of maturity, the world of work, of duty, of culture, of progress—to the future. We often made fun of them and played jokes on them, but in our hearts we trusted them. The idea of authority, which they represented, was associated in our minds with a greater insight and a manlier wisdom. But the first death we saw shattered this belief. We had to recognize that our generation was more to be trusted than theirs. They surpassed us only in phrases and in cleverness. The first bombardment showed us our mistake, and under it the world as they had taught it to us broke in pieces.

While they continued to write and talk, we saw the wounded and dying. While they taught that duty to one's country is the greatest thing, we already knew that death-throes are stronger. But for all that we were no mutineers, no deserters, no cowards—they were very free with all these expressions. We loved our country as much as they; we went courageously into every action; but also we distinguished the false from the true, we had suddenly learned to see. And we saw that there was nothing of their world left. We were all at once terribly alone; and alone we must see it through.

* * *

Before going over to see Kemmerich we pack up his things: he will need them on the way back.

In the dressing-station there is great activity; it reeks as ever of carbolic, ether, and sweat. Most of us are accustomed to this in the billets, but here it makes one feel faint. We ask for Kemmerich. He lies in a large room and receives us with feeble expressions of joy and helpless agitation. While he was unconscious someone had stolen his watch.

Müller shakes his head: "I always told you that nobody should carry as good a watch as that."

Müller is rather crude and tactless, otherwise he would hold his tongue, for anybody can see that Kemmerich will never come out of this place again. Whether he finds his watch or not will make no difference. At the most one will only be able to send it to his people.

"How goes it, Franz?" asks Kropp.

Kemmerich's head sinks.

"Not so bad . . . but I have such a damned pain in my foot."

We look at his bed covering. His leg lies under a wire basket. The bed covering arches over it. I kick Müller on the shin, for he is just about to tell Kemmerich what the orderlies told us outside: that Kemmerich has lost his foot. The leg is amputated. He looks ghastly, yellow, and wan. In his face there are already the strained lines that we know so well, we have seen them now hundreds of times. They are not so much lines as marks. Under the skin the life no longer pulses, it has already pressed out to the boundaries of the body. Death is working through from within. It already has command in the eyes. Here lies our comrade, Kemmerich, who a little while ago was roasting horse-flesh with us and squatting in the shell-holes. He it is still and yet it is not he any longer. His features have become uncertain and faint, like a photographic plate on which two pictures have been taken. Even his voice sounds like ashes.

I think of the time when we went away. His mother, a good plump matron, brought him to the station. She wept continually, her face was bloated and swollen. Kemmerich felt embarrassed, for she was the least composed of all; she simply dissolved into fat and water. Then she caught sight of me and took hold of my arm again and again, and implored me to look after Franz out there. Indeed he did have a face like a child, and such frail bones that after four weeks pack-carrying he already had flat feet. But how can a man look after anyone in the field!

"Now you will soon be going home," says Kropp. "You

would have had to wait at least three or four months for your leave.''

Kemmerich nods. I cannot bear to look at his hands, they are like wax. Under the nails is the dirt of the trenches, it shows through blue-black like poison. It strikes me that these nails will continue to grow like long fantastic cellar-plants long after Kemmerich breathes no more. I see the picture before me. They twist themselves into corkscrews and grow and grow, and with them the hair on the decayed skull, just like grass in a good soil, just like grass, how can it be possible—

Müller leans over. "We have brought your things, Franz."

Kemmerich signs with his hand. "Put them under the bed."

Müller does so. Kemmerich starts on again about the watch. How can one calm him without making him suspicious?

Müller reappears with a pair of airman's boots. They are fine English boots of soft, yellow leather which reach to the knee and lace all the way—they are things to be coveted.

Müller is delighted at the sight of them. He matches their soles against his own clumsy boots and says: "Will you be taking them with you, Franz?"

We all three have the same thought; even if he should get better, he would be able to use only one—they are no use to him. But as things are now it is a pity that they should stay here; the orderlies will of course grab them as soon as he is dead.

"Won't you leave them with us?" Müller repeats.

Kemmerich doesn't want to. They are his most prized possessions.

"Well, we could exchange," suggests Müller again. "Out here one can make some use of them." Still Kemmerich is not to be moved.

I tread on Müller's foot; reluctantly he puts the fine boots back again under the bed.

We talk a little more and then take our leave.

"Cheerio, Franz."

I promise him to come back in the morning. Müller talks of doing so too. He is thinking of the lace-up boots and means to be on the spot.

Kemmerich groans. He is feverish. We get hold of an orderly outside and ask him to give Kemmerich a dose of morphia.

He refuses. "If we were to give morphia to everyone we would have to have tubs full—"

"You only attend to officers properly," says Kropp viciously.

I hastily intervene and give him a cigarette. He takes it.

"Are you usually allowed to give it, then?" I ask him.

He is annoyed. "If you don't think so, then why do you ask?"

I press a couple more cigarettes into his hand. "Do us the favour—"

"Well, all right," he says.

Kropp goes in with him. He doesn't trust him and wants to see. We wait outside.

Müller returns to the subject of the boots. "They would fit me perfectly. In these boots I get blister after blister. Do you think he will last till tomorrow after drill? If he passes out in the night, we know where the boots—"

Kropp returns. "Do you think—?" he asks.

"Done for," says Müller emphatically.

We go back to the huts. I think of the letter that I must

write to-morrow to Kemmerich's mother. I am freezing. I could do with a tot of rum. Müller pulls up some grass and chews it. Suddenly little Kropp throws his cigarette away, stamps on it savagely, and looking round him with a broken and distracted face, stammers: "Damned shit, the damned shit!"

We walk on for a long time. Kropp has calmed himself; we understand: he sees red, out here every man gets like that sometime.

"What has Kantorek written to you?" Müller asks him.

He laughs. "We are the Iron Youth."

We all three smile bitterly. Kropp rails: he is glad that he can speak.

Yes, that's the way they think, these hundred thousand Kantoreks! Iron Youth. Youth! We are none of us more than twenty years old. But young? Youth? That is long ago. We are old folk.

ANATOMY OF ME
by Fannie Hurst

In the twenties and thirties readers wept and sentamentalized over Fannie Hurst's novels, particularly Back Street, *and* Imitation of Life, *which became popular films of their time. While she was still quite young* The Saturday Evening Post, The Delineator, *and other magazines were bidding for her short stories. Her father wrote her: "You are a very young girl to be meeting with so much success. Needless to say, your mother and I are gratified. I consider it the finest thing that has happened in my lifetime. But I urge you to bear in mind that modesty and proper demeanor are needed now as never before. Remember, success does not necessarily last forever. Enjoy it, but build your character to meet life as it comes. Take care of your health, because not even success can take its place. People stop me on the street to congratulate me, and you can imagine your mother's pleasure in your daily letters."*

Fannie Hurst's father was steady and temperate, her mother stormy and mercurial. Because of her mother much of Fannie's early life was unhappy but she would never admit to not loving "Mama." She felt it blasphemous when some years later a chance acquaintance, a member of the English peerage, said to her, "I hate my mother."

WHEN the time came for me to enter high school we became a household divided.

Mama wanted me to attend one of the town's select private schools, Mary Institute or Harperly Hall. Papa was for Central High School.

Inwardly I leaned in his direction, but somehow when he put it into words it set up in me that mysterious amalgam, family antagonism.

I am willing to scrape and stint myself, blazed Mama, but I don't intend to do it on my child.

The public schools of the United States are good enough for me, contended Papa.

And what about the riffraff your daughter may encounter? I want her to have the best.

I have nothing more to add, said Papa, and retired behind his newspaper.

Despite his unusually decisive manner, Mama held out. I was entered at Harperly Hall. It seemed more like a handsome private residence, which it had once been. Potted palms everywhere, framed Anderson prints of the Colosseum by Moonlight, Michelangelo's David, and Murillo's Madonna and Child, following the wall space of the great winding staircase.

The headmistress, a large woman with a wide shelf of bosom, and salt-and-pepper hair which she wore in a high stern pile, received us.

She had my application and school grades before her.

Mr. Hurst's occupation? Age. Grandparents, maternal and paternal, names and places of birth. And here it came! Religion?

Jewish, replied Mama, as if she were biting off a thread.

The headmistress's pen paused an almost imperceptible second and so did my breathing, then both proceeded.

What else could Mama have said! But, punily, I would have given anything not to have had her say that word to this lady whose professional graciousness seemed to curdle for the instant and then turn back into cream.

She questioned me. Yes, I liked school. English and

history were my favorite studies. No, I don't ride horseback. Yes, I hoped to learn French.

Sports? I didn't know anything about them, except tennis. Travel in the United States or Europe? Only in America. Where? Hamilton, Ohio. Have you ever been to Vicksburg, your father's birthplace? No.

It occurred to me how little I knew of Papa's youth. Mama's family was near and dear. Papa's somehow remote.

The headmistress then talked tuition and all the extras with Mama. Harmony, horseback riding, voice, fencing, concerts, textbooks; and then said that we would hear from her, as the school was quite crowded and the waiting list long.

On the way home, Mama was explosive. The nerve of her! You would think we had come asking something for nothing. Where, how, and why were we born? What has that got to do with education? I guess your father was right, only don't let him know I said so.

I felt one major burning apprehension but could not bring myself to speak about it. Girls from the boulevards and the big houses in the outlying towns came there for culture. I suddenly wanted Harperly, except for that burning and challenging apprehension.

As we neared home, Mama, still fuming, spoke it out for me.

And on top of it all, I think she was *richus*.

When Mama used that word, it grated against me like sandpaper.

To have *richus*, I knew from Mama's and my Aunts' lips, was to have "race prejudice," a phrase which never failed to strike dread and humiliation into me.

I did not say as much to Mama, but I wondered if I

would be accepted. If only that terrible question had not been asked. What did it matter? Neither by appearance nor manner were we typed. The horrid little thoughts crawled all through me, and on they crawled.

A week later we were notified of my acceptance, and I entered Harperly Hall the following autumn. It proved a heartbreaking experience of short duration. From the beginning, my separateness from the Harperly girls, even though it had nothing to do with creed, asserted itself.

I doubt if it was due to anything more than my own self-conscious aloofness, quickened by the fact, soon apparent, that I had little in common with these girls. They were Schwachts, van Blarkoms, Baumgartens, Kunkles, brewery, banking, real estate, railroad names in our city. The Kunkle twins had been registered for Vassar the day they were born. The van Blarkom girl lived in one of the finest Victorian mansions in Vandeventer Place. Most of the pupils arrived at Harperly Hall in family limousines. They knew one another out of Harperly, attended the same dancing classes, conducted privately in the ballroom of the Kunkle home in Westmoreland Place, and went with their families to the same summer resorts, Bar Harbor or Kennebunkport, Maine, or Europe.

It is not improbable that nothing more or less than my contrast to these plainly dressed girls was responsible for some of my isolation. Mama sent me out in clothes geared, so she thought, to Harperly. I arrived my first day in plaid, the skirt ruffled to the waist, and an enormous hair bow of corresponding plaid accenting my high pompadour. Shoes, patent leather with plaid tops.

It had been a lovely outfit when I left home, but at Harperly I was hot in it, bothered in it, and suddenly furious with Mama.

To be sure, there was something at Harperly I lacked at home. Certain amenities, I suppose, but they did little if anything for the wide lonesome places within my growing self.

Mama said: No wonder you're lonesome, you don't mix.

The dark word "lonely" had not yet moved into my consciousness. It was not that I was lonesome at Harperly for the girls who did not make up to me. I was lonely for what Harperly could not give me. For what my kind of life could not give me . . . It was rather the beginnings in me of that endemic ailment of the lonely spirit and youth . . . that indefinable hunger . . .

I endured silent and miserable weeks at Harperly, Mama's eagle eye probing.

Either you don't feel well or something is bothering you.

Please, Mama, I tell you I'm all right.

It's that school. You don't like it.

Did I say anything!

What don't you like?

But I do.

Fannie, is there *richus*?

That dreadful word again!

No.

I guess your father was right. I made a mistake in sending you there.

At the end of the third month I broke down.

Don't make me go back there. What I want isn't there!

What do you want?

I don't know, only I know it isn't there.

Five hundred dollars for tuition and now she discovers that what she wants isn't there . . . .

I entered high school a semester late, with private lessons to help make up for the delayed start.

At the time, St. Louis, a city of six hundred thousand, boasted one high school, a huge red brick structure, midtown. Fourteen hundred pupils streamed through its wide corridors.

Here were the masses! I swam into their midst like a delighted duck into new waters.

Subconsciously, I suppose, I was already seeking the people, and Harperly Hall had been a matter of persons.

At Central High you said "tomato" and "can't" without the broad *a*. I wore my plaid dress with the ruffles and it drew admiring eyes. In contrast to Harperly Hall, the teaching staff seemed alive and stimulating. No one heeded whether you crossed your legs, or saw to it that the young ladies were hatted and gloved before leaving the building.

Almost immediately, one of the male teachers, a Mr. Heide, history department, became my secret passion and inner excitement. I don't believe even when I tried to capture his interest by laborious attempts at originality when called upon in class that he ever gave me a sustained look.

Mama said: You would think you were going to the Veiled Prophets Ball the way you waste time in front of the looking glass dressing for school.

The sweet pain of Mr. Heide moved through my first weeks of Central High. I thought of life for us both. I thought of death for us both. Death, where is thy sting, with Mr. Heide . . . .

Mama said and said: That Harperly Hall with its *richus*. I'm going to ask them to refund the tuition money I paid in advance.

Papa put his foot down. Rose, you cannot do that. Business is not conducted that way.

It's not the money, it's the principle, insisted Mama stubbornly.

But there was something in Papa's voice and frown that Mama did not further controvert.

For years afterward, whenever we passed Harperly Hall, Mama would let go: Robbers!

GROWING UP
by David Ignatow

David Ignatow is an innovative poet of plain, authentic speech. He writes both lyric and prose poems on subjects that take in the range of human experience. By turns gentle, violent, satirical, he uses "quietly astute but not obscure language to reveal the affinities and hidden significances in the everyday and the overlooked." He was awarded the Bollingen Prize in Poetry for distinguished work. His numerous other awards include the Shelley Award of the Poetry Society of America and a Guggenheim Fellowship. This selection is from his book Whisper to the Earth.

THESE were among my first thoughts on earth: I had been placed here as some kind of reward, given the gift of being what I was, and I loved my bike, praising it for moving at the command of my pedaling, and steering in the right direction at my touch. The sidewalk lay flat and still, expecting the bike. It, too, cooperated with the powers that be, and no one stood in the bike's path to topple me over. The wind upon my face was like the hand of approval. Where then was my change hiding, my hidden change?

I never thought the bike betrayed me, nor the sidewalk, nor the wind, but now I see them simply as means, and the betrayer is me. I cannot call the bike an emissary. It is a tool, the sidewalk is a path, the wind a current of air. We are no longer communicating that I'm aware of, but what does it matter, I tell myself, so long as I am free to use all these for my delight; but I am alone in my pleasures. I am not the child of anyone, for, as I watch myself growing up, the bike shrinks in size and the sidewalk fills with cracks and bumps; the wind on my face in cold weather chills me, and when I eat I know it is because of appetite.

I have become something else, no longer at one with bike, sidewalk and wind. I can feel cold, hunger, appetite, the self and all that this means—because the bike never is hungry, nor does the sidewalk ever have to go to bed, and sometimes the wind stops blowing and for me does not exist, which, earlier, would have frightened me about myself, while the wind never is frightened; it never speaks about itself, as I am beginning to speak about myself, and so I know there is something about me very different. Sometimes I am panicky about it, but more often I am glad because I have still another thing to turn to in pleasure, and that is this self which is always with me, but I am alone because a tree has begun to look lonely to me standing by itself, whereas once I had thought it beautiful, saying what I felt about myself too—that I was, that we both were. Now the tree looks lonely, but I know that that also is my thinking, and the thinking is my pleasure and my burden too. I am all alone, and so I turn to another like myself and find him happy to turn to me.

And now we have begun to differ about the games we should be playing or the places to visit on our bikes or the time to go home for dinner. I become lonely again, my self needing to be defended as my only absolute friend and sharer, but my friend and I exchange smiles often and talk together with gentleness and teasing and wait for the voices of our parents to call us separately to dinner.

REBELLION
by Ruth Harnden

---

*"Rebellion," other than in an ironic sense, is a curious title
for this story. At most, it concerns an aborted rebellion.
Written in the mid-Fifties it is light-years away from the
student rebellions of the Sixties and Seventies. Borrowing
from its closing lines, it could better have been called
"Hunter" or, indeed, "Huntress."*

*For a brief time, Susie, an affluent, well-positioned girl,
away from her own country, forgets social status and
income brackets to enjoy the fresh, natural freedom of
friendship with someone with whom she has common
interests. She finds herself asking questions of her new-
found friend even when he is not there, sure proof of
friendship.*

*She has the courage to question her way of life, but not
the courage to act upon the answers. Nor is she skillful
enough—for skillful should one read willing?—to save the
friendship. The real coming of age is not seen in Susie, but
in Jimmy.*

It is interesting that the story was published in Town and
Country, *a paradigm of sleek, expensive, fashionable
magazines. The story might less likely be written today; the
Susies are still with us, but there are also more real rebels.*

LAST year, at fifteen, she had been a private person, and
next year at seventeen, so far as she knew, she might expect
to be so again. Only this year she seemed to have been
thrust into the public domain, made to feel as conspicuous,
and at the same time anonymous, as though she were
ludicrously fat, or suffered from any condition that was

the accepted butt of stale, universal humor brought out again and again with the zeal of discovery. *Sweet sixteen*.

"What a lovely thought, Dr. Mulcahey, or Mr. Byrne, or Colonel McGuire," she would have liked to say, looking stonily back into their archly smiling faces. "Did it just come to you? Or is it a quotation, perhaps?" Or she might simply say, "I feel sour, thank you. Quite sour!" and turn and walk out of the alien, enormous room filled with the aged or the aging who had no respect for her whatsoever, only a terrible, stripping curiosity.

She was either interested in people—deeply, passionately—or she barely saw them at all. But now she began to wonder whether she, too, was doomed to arrive one day at this peculiar, repulsive condition in which interest had given place to a dull, sly curiosity for something that had lost all reality.

An only child, too much of her life had been lived in an adult world. As a result she was mentally precocious, which she knew, and emotionally somewhat in arrears, which she was only beginning to know. The latter awareness manifested itself in a nameless impatience. She had become very critical, was frequently short-tempered, and was ridden by a continual unrest. It was partly on this account that her parents had chosen this season to ship her off to her uncle and his wife, who had no children of their own and an "interesting life" in the diplomatic service.

"You're a born rebel, Susie," her uncle had begun to say almost from the day she arrived, and it did seem as if her unrest was a kind of imminent rebellion that any minute, or any day, she would find the strength to express properly. In the meantime if came out in small intellectual attacks fairly well within the bounds of good manners.

"What's the matter with having *both* central heating and

open fires?'' she wanted to know when it was explained to her that many people could afford central heating, that some had even had it installed and then never connected it because they preferred the intimate comfort of fires in every room.

"Why don't they pasteurize their milk?'' she demanded when she learned that it was customarily left raw, and that tuberculosis was rife in the country. But the chief object of her attack was the terrible inequality, the lack of democracy. At first it had seemed to her that people here must be wealthier than the same sort of people at home, but her aunt put her straight on that. "Heavens, no!'' she said, "it's just the other way around. This is a poor country, and America's one of the richest.'' It was the servants, Susan explained. "Oh—that!'' her aunt said. "But they're so cheap here. We can get four servants for the price of one in the States.''

"You mean,'' Susan pointed out unsparingly, "that a great many people have nothing so that a very few can have everything?''

"Highty tighty,'' her uncle broke in at that. "A disciple of Marx?''

"No,'' she said coldly, "but if I lived here I'd probably become one.''

"Of course it spoils us dreadfully,'' her aunt admitted with one of her gestures of delicate, side-stepping surrender that no one could mistake for defeat. She was a small, fastidious woman who managed to look fragile and feminine even in the most robust tweeds. At an age when she should have faded, the soft moist Irish weather had given her skin a renascent bloom. She kept her graying hair short and exquisitely groomed, and had never neglected the care of her hands. Beside her Susan felt a little gross—over-grown and under-organized. She was likely to do clumsy things, drop a teacup or a walking stick, stumble over a rug, although she was normally well co-ordinated. But more devastating than her aunt's person was her bland, humorless sweet temper that could uncurdle the sourest wit, that blunted the edge of argument so effectively that even discussion died stillborn.

"We have to take things as we find them," her uncle had said in a terminating voice. He found them very comfortable indeed and this knowledge only increased Susan's critical impatience. They were old and they had given up. They would rather be comfortable than alive. And being very uncomfortable, she told herself that she would rather be alive. But still she had this uncertainty of her own life; not that it had ended, but that it was unbegun. During that single, suspended week of freedom on the boat it had seemed likely at any moment to begin. She had played Ping-pong and danced a few times with an older man, a Swiss who traveled for Du Pont. He was perhaps thirty and had given her a heady sense of imminent danger. But nothing at all had happened, and in recollection the whole thing gave her the feeling she got from developing a film that turned out to have been light-struck in the camera so that even her anticipation had been meaningless. She told herself in honest hindsight that he had treated her like a nice kid, as though she wore her obstructing innocence like a brand. And if she did—if that were the case—then how could anything happen? And if nothing happened, then how was it lost?

There were only two things in which she was uncritically content because in them she could be wholly involved as nothing else in life any longer seemed willing or able to involve her. She loved to drive a car and to ride a horse, particularly the latter. Occasionally she would ride badly, failing to quite manage the horse, and at these times she would need to take out the car, to drive it with a combination of abandon and precision that almost restored her self-esteem. But it wasn't the same thing, and she knew it with a glancing, secret contempt for the inert manageability of machines. You had no relationship with a machine, and along with the speed and the exhilarating presence of potential danger, which removed her restlessness, it was exactly the *relationship* she craved. The lonelier she felt in this alien place, in the embarrassment of her conspicuous youth, the more she needed it.

Dublin was a good place to have come to if you liked riding. Diplomatically it was not a brilliant post, but for that reason neither was it taxing. After some ten years her aunt and uncle had relaxed into a close resemblance, at least, of the amiable, indolent ways of the country born and bred. Their frequent receptions had preserved a formality—in the dress, in the food and liquor served, and in the conversational interchange or the musical intrusions. These gatherings usually showed, too, a considerable urban variety of guests. But their weekly At Homes had pretty well boiled down to the informal hard-riding set, who might occasionally talk of their gardens but never got any further away than that from the turf. Prosperous farmers or titled gentry, they had identical hard-planed, weather-burned faces and conducted their conversations in an identical manner, the voices booming, the diction blurred. Men and women dressed alike, in the tough, unregarded tweeds that never seemed to reach retirement and it even appeared to Susan that there was little other difference between them, except that the women were apt to have deeper voices, and their faces were frequently harder.

Through this florid, shouting, unintelligible crowd she would move every Thursday afternoon at the same hours, passing buttered bread or refilling teacups and saying, "No, I don't hunt," for the hundredth time, or "No, I haven't been out yet." "Hunt?" or "Started to hunt yet?" was offered to her over and over, or perhaps simply "Been out yet?" which she learned quite soon could have, in their changeless context, only the one reference.

She had done a little jumping at home, but only over the simplest hurdles. After a trial hour in the field with her uncle it had been decided that she was not, or not yet, up to the banks. Evidently an Irish invention, the banks were towering, beveled mounds of earth. She had no notion of their actual height but would have guessed it at no less than twelve feet. Put at the bank, the horse would leap and then scramble up the angled sides, pause briefly on the leveled top, and then plunge headlong to the ground at the far side. It was the downward leap that appalled her, that sent her frightened, betraying hands to the saddle, and that formed the basis for her uncle's decision.

"You'll go out every morning," he told her, "with one of the grooms." In point of fact their horses were supplied by the nearby army post and the "grooms" were any of the enlisted men whose services were an added diplomatic courtesy on demand. The actual arrangements were made by her aunt on the telephone. Any course might be determined by her husband, but its execution, the applied diplomacy, usually fell to her lot. She had to a high degree that capacity for verbal indirection which results in the most unmistakable directness.

After the first few days the stolid, middle-aged sergeant her aunt had unerringly selected, sight unseen, was unexpectedly hospitalized with a ruptured appendix. On Saturday morning, at the customary hours, a young corporal came up with the horses. He was a thin, tallish boy who looked to be little older than Susan herself. While he adjusted her stirrups, standing at her horse's head, she examined his stark boy's face with the fine pink girlish complexion, the intent, impersonal gray eyes, and it came to her that he knew all about horses and that he knew nothing else. As far as people, as far as Life was concerned, he was way back there at the beginning with herself. Out of the simplicity of this bond and this freedom she began to talk to him as easily as she could talk to no one else in this place, not even thinking how to begin, as she had had to think with the sergeant so that she'd never begun at all.

"First I thought I'd never be able to handle a horse on a snaffle," she told him. "At home we use the curb, too, you know. Or if it's a single rein, then it's the curb. That's what they use in the West. That's what the cowboys use."

"For a fact?" he said, interested, his intent, unconcealing eyes coming up to hers without embarrassment or curiosity even, except for the words she was saying. "Anyone could hold a horse on a curb," he said then, swinging into his own saddle.

"I know it," she said just as naturally. "And I still don't know how I'd handle him on a snaffle if he wanted to run." He laughed at that. "Why would you be wantin' to hold him in that case?" he asked her. "Sure he'd have to stop when he got to the sea." That made her laugh, and presently they were cantering across the sere, stubbled grass of Phoenix Park as if they'd been doing it every morning of their lives.

There was no end to what they found to say without ever leaving the subject of horses and riding. He was teaching her a great deal but she was able to tell him a lot too. "This is the way the cowboys ride," she'd say, sitting to the trot, "taking the jolts on their stomachs. Of course they prefer a single-foot," she might add, "and anyone can sit to that."

"You can train 'em to that sometimes," he'd say, "sending 'em against the bit. But you've a better chance if they're inclined that way."

"But I like to post," she told him. "I *enjoy* it." She was even able to confess to him that she was scared of the banks. "I grabbed the saddle," she said, looking him straight in the eye, daring him to accept this and still go on knowing her.

"You've a good seat," he told her, looking straight back as if there were no disgrace standing between them. "Just leave it to the horse. Give him his head and leave it to him."

"I'd have to stop when I got to the ground?" she asked him, and they laughed together over this for a long time.

There was so much to say that by the end of the week she found herself talking to him when he wasn't there, asking him questions or explaining something to him, or going back over some point that had come up the day before, or that morning.

He never called her "Miss" the way the sergeant did, and still he'd never used her name either. It was just "you" or else he was simply talking as if she were anyone, or a number of people. But she knew that it wasn't like that. If it were he could have used her name. She knew this without knowing that she knew it until the day that he used her name.

They had gone up into the hills that morning for another try at the banks. "We'll take 'em together," he suggested. "Just give the horses the office and relax." But she decided that she'd rather, the first time, he waited for her on the far side, and finally he agreed to do that. It was on the far side, reaching the ground, that her horse stumbled and then fell. It seemed to her, reviewing it afterward, and even dimly at the time, that she'd barely felt the earth with her shoulder before he was off his horse and standing over her saying, "Susie, are you hurt? Are you hurt?" and it wasn't only her name but the sharp pain in his voice that she heard. "You're shakin," he said, helping her up, holding her against the tension of his arm. "Are you all right?"

"Just dirty, I guess," she said, trying to laugh. He took out his handkerchief and dabbed at her forehead, her cheekbones, but when he got to her mouth he stopped and stuffed the handkerchief back in his pocket. "The thing to do," he said, speaking quickly in an oddly light voice, "is to get straight back on again. You've always got to do that at once or you'll maybe never do it again. Come along now," he said, busying himself with the two sets of reins he'd caught up through his arm, "up and at it again. You did fine—just fine! It was only for the beast stumblin' or you'd be in the saddle now easy as sittin' in the barn." It was like the time on the boat, and it was entirely different, because this time the nothing that had happened had happened to both of them.

It was more than a week before her aunt caught up to the fact that a substitution had been made in her plans. She happened to drive up from town just as Susan had got into the house, so of course she met the corporal coming down the driveway leading the second, riderless horse. "Hullo. Was that Sergeant Blair?" she asked casually, standing in the hall stripping the string gloves from her hands. It was a minute before Susan could think who Sergeant Blair was. "Oh!" she said then, remembering, "Oh, he's in the hospital. His appendix broke. Two weeks ago, I guess it was. Or maybe it was ten days." "Really?" her aunt said, examining herself in the hall mirror. "As long as that?" "It seems much longer," Susan told her innocently, out of the moment's disarmed surprise. "It seems like a month at least that I've been riding with Jimmy."

"Really?" her aunt said again, having turned from the mirror now, and after a minute the irresolution in her face, studying Susan's, resolved itself in a smile. "How nice that you've made a friend," she said. "We must meet him. Would you like to ask him for dinner one night?"

"Oh, no!" Susan said out of the unexamined but certain instinct of an animal sensing an ambushed trap. "We just like to talk about horses," she said quickly, reaching for some protection of this thing that was hers alone in this alien place, this estranging time. "In that case," her aunt said sweetly, "just have him in Thursday," and she put her gloves down on the table, the tough leather palms turned up, and went into the morning room.

She ought to have thought quicker, and further. She ought to have seen past the logic of Thursday when everyone who came talked about horses. But the moment was past and she was caught. She was caught beyond escape in her aunt's logic, and in her graciousness—switching at once to the thing that Susan might prefer.

She waited until the end of their ride on Thursday and then getting off at the house, handing him her reins, she gave it to him the way it was: not a thing that needed accepting, or could possibly be refused. "Aunt Helen wants you to come for tea. About four they usually come. Any time between four and five. I'll see you then," she told him, and turned and went into the house without waiting to see what it might be that finally found its way to the surface of his intent, uncomplicated face.

It was perhaps four-thirty and everyone had gathered when she saw him at the threshold to the room, his young face looking exposed and raw hanging in uncertainty above the poise of her aunt's head. "I'm sure you know the army people already," her aunt was saying when she got to them, "though I'm afraid they're all aged career men."

"Hullo," Susan said, searching his face for any sign that he too, had heard how her aunt had taken away with the one word what she had given to the other. There was nothing to be read but a certain wariness when he said, "How do you do?" speaking as distinctly as if the words belonged to a foreign tongue. "Introduce Corporal Faley to the Colonel, darling," her aunt said, "and to Captain Sweeney and to Major Cunningham. And then get him a cup of tea," and she moved away.

"Come on," Susan said, not looking at him any longer, her face set in the stubborn, reckless hope that something might still be saved.

Colonel McGuire opened his mouth and barked something that might have been an acknowledgment of the introduction in this room where introductions were not made, and might as well have been the beginning of the story he launched into at once: some incident from the week before when he'd been out with the Killing Kildares. No one needed to ask the corporal which hunt he rode with, or even if he hunted at all. No one seemed to feel the need to ask him anything at all, and after a minute Susan said, "I'll get you some tea," and moved away from the identical faces which had assumed a further identity now. Without exception they were united at this moment in the bland, incurious conviction that anyone who was at all worth knowing they knew already.

She never did get him the tea although she made three tries going back after another cup when the first one was taken by Mr. Kavenaugh, stopping her in the middle of the room. Everyone all at once was determined to stop her, to engage her in conversation, to deflect her eyes searching the room for his face, from Old Lady Closs, who wanted to know if she was going to any of the dances, to Mr. Byrne, who expressed a sudden interest in her political views. She knew she was being wooed, and she knew why. She knew exactly what was going on, and had known from her aunt's first words. But when she was stopped with the third cup, her stubborn frustration went down to helpless defeat. She felt it go as certainly as she might have watched a sentinel leaving his post. But it was no less gone for that.

She was one of them now. No longer anonymous, and briefly comical, she was addressed, consulted, attended. She might have been grown-up; she might have been eighteen. And she began to hear her own voice rising on the competitive tide, her own words running together in expedient haste. It was a kind of intoxication, heady and numbing at once. She had really forgotten Jimmy's presence when her aunt's voice broke the spell at last. She thought Susan'ought to know Corporal Faley was leaving and surely she wanted to see him out.

He was standing alone in the hall, his back to the broad mirror that alone preserved the image of his integrity—the squared competent shoulders, the stark attention of the head. "I'm sorry—" she began, and then she stopped, and it was perhaps after all the only thing she had to say.

"That's all right," he said very quickly, possibly to spare her or perhaps to spare himself further. Into the unaware, youthful dignity of his face had come the beginning of adult confusion. His eyes shifted to some focus beyond her. "I'll . . . " his lean, assured boy's hand that was so certain on a horse's mouth lifted in a faltering gesture, as though it moved toward a cap he wasn't wearing. "I'll bring the horses 'round in the morning," he said in a final definition of the status they had assigned him. Without looking at her again he crossed the hall, treading the carpet lightly, and let himself out the front door.

For a minute she stood alone in the hall. Behind her, across the wide house, the shouting unintelligible crowd sounded like one voice now, single as the voice of the pack. Her rebellion flared briefly, a last time. *Why did you let them*? she asked of the door that had closed behind him. If he hadn't fallen into their trap; if he hadn't accepted that identity they gave him; if he hadn't proved their point—her rebellion guttered and died because she had proved their point herself, as well. She belonged to the hunted no longer. She had become a member of the hunt.